THE COMPLETE MOTHER GOOSE

ILLUSTRATIONS

BY

ETHEL FRANKLIN BETTS

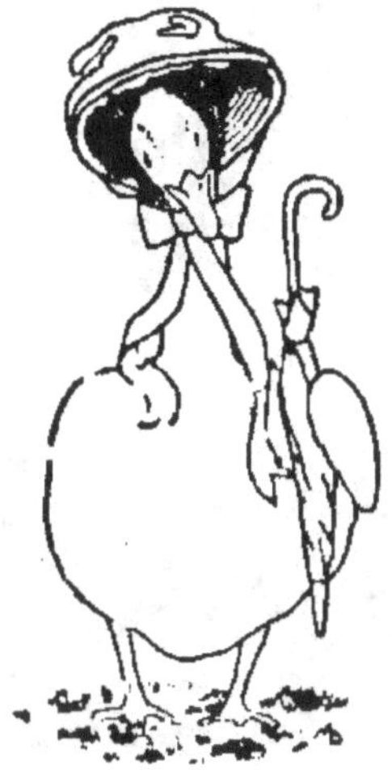

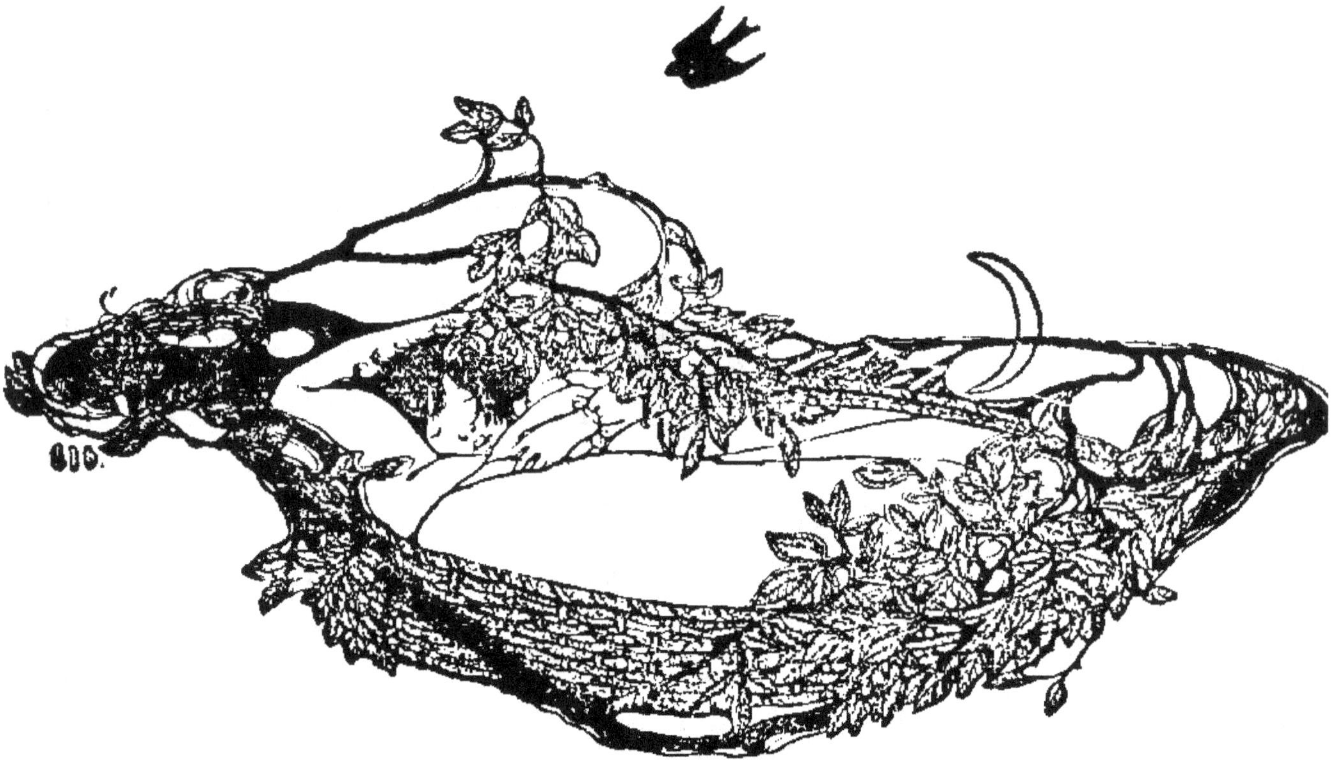

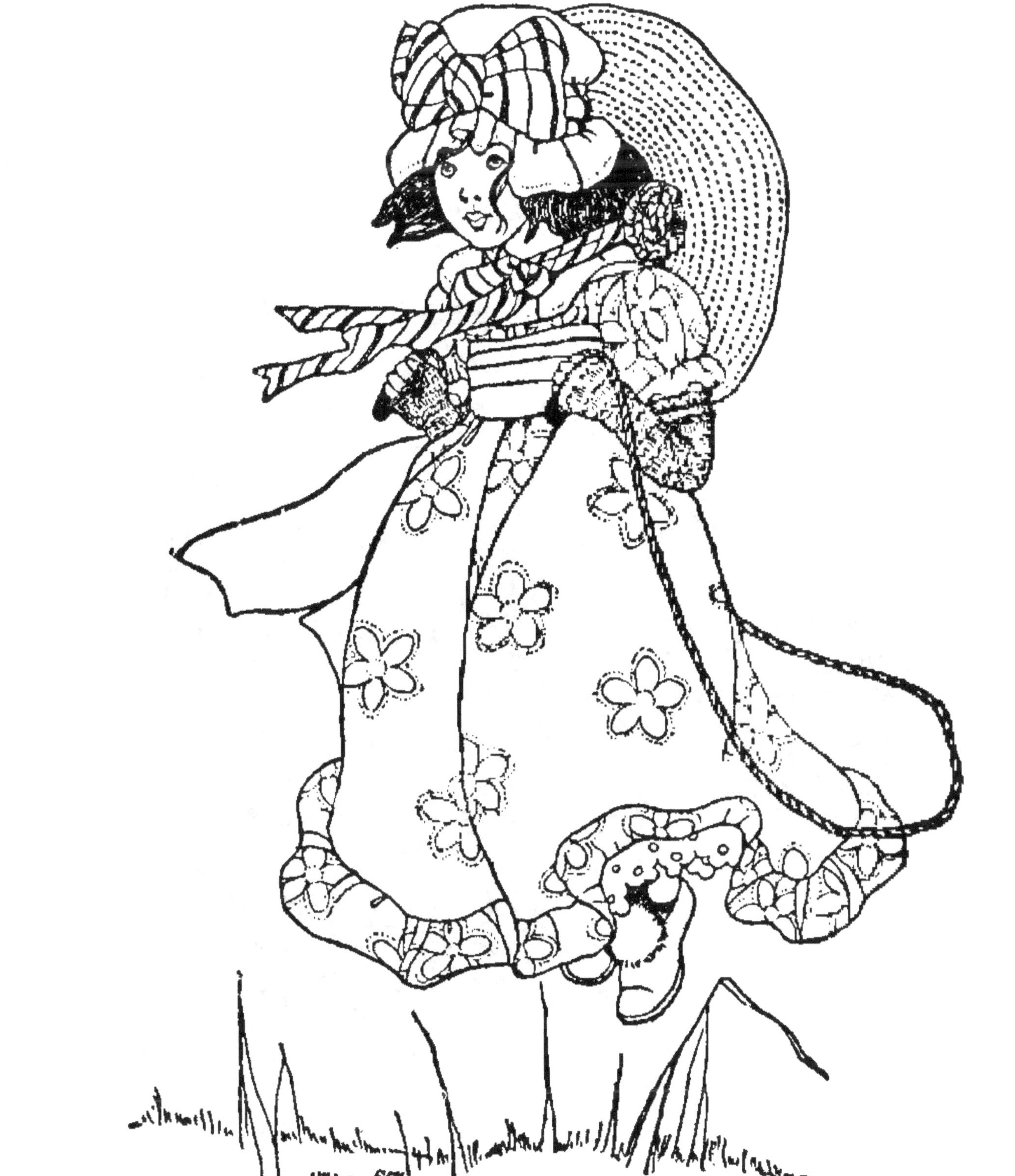

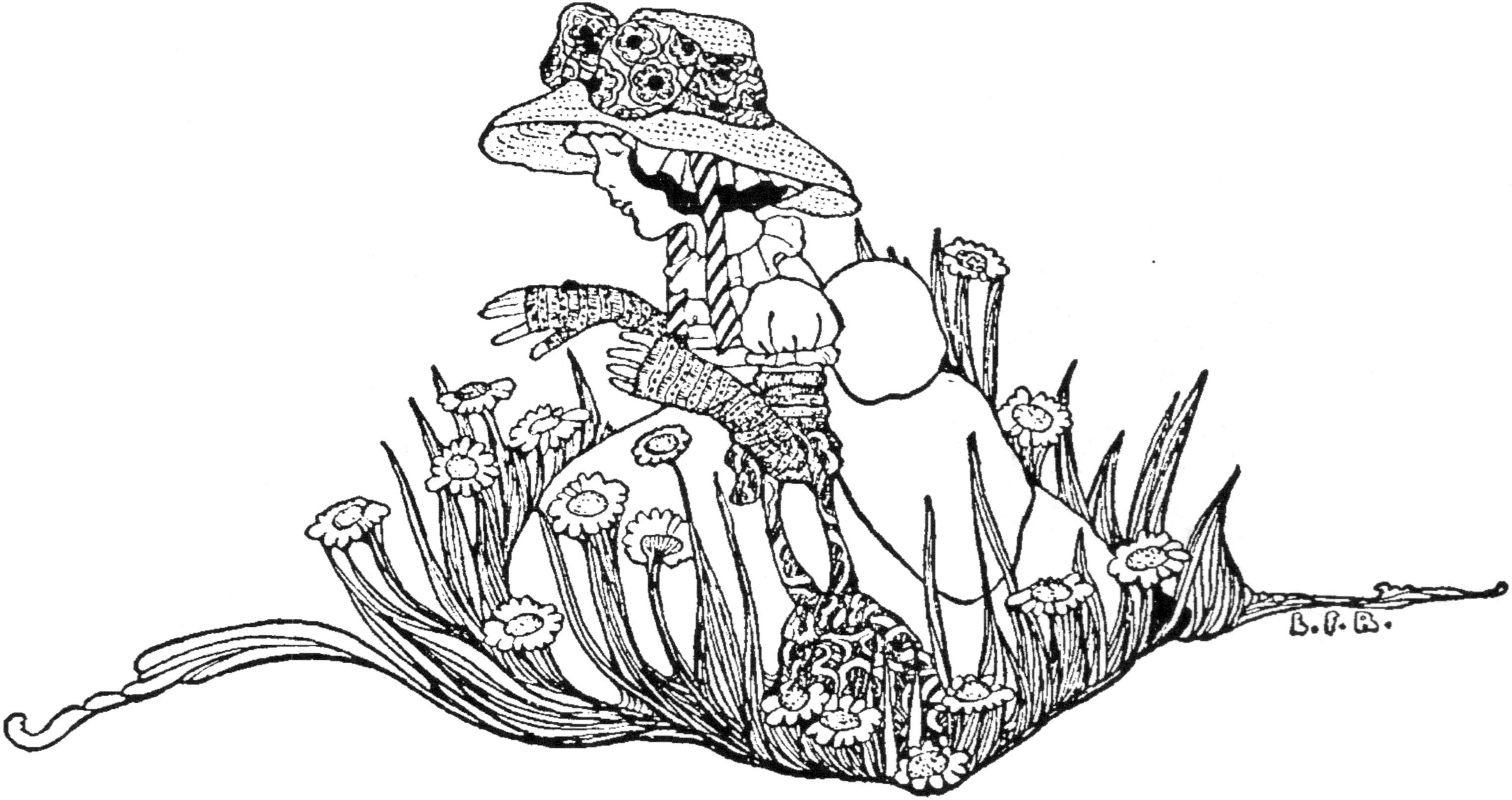

Lady Bug, Lady Bug

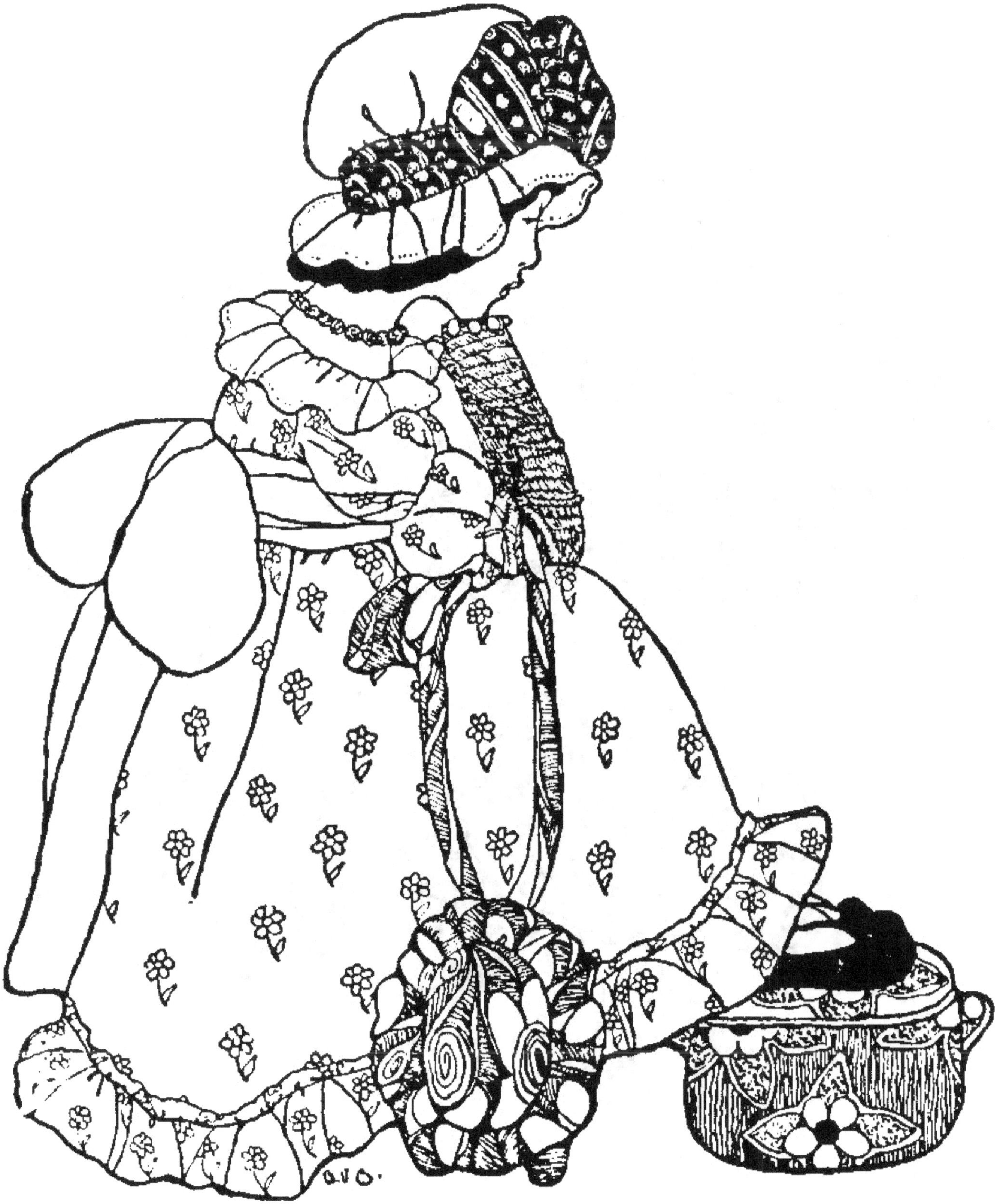

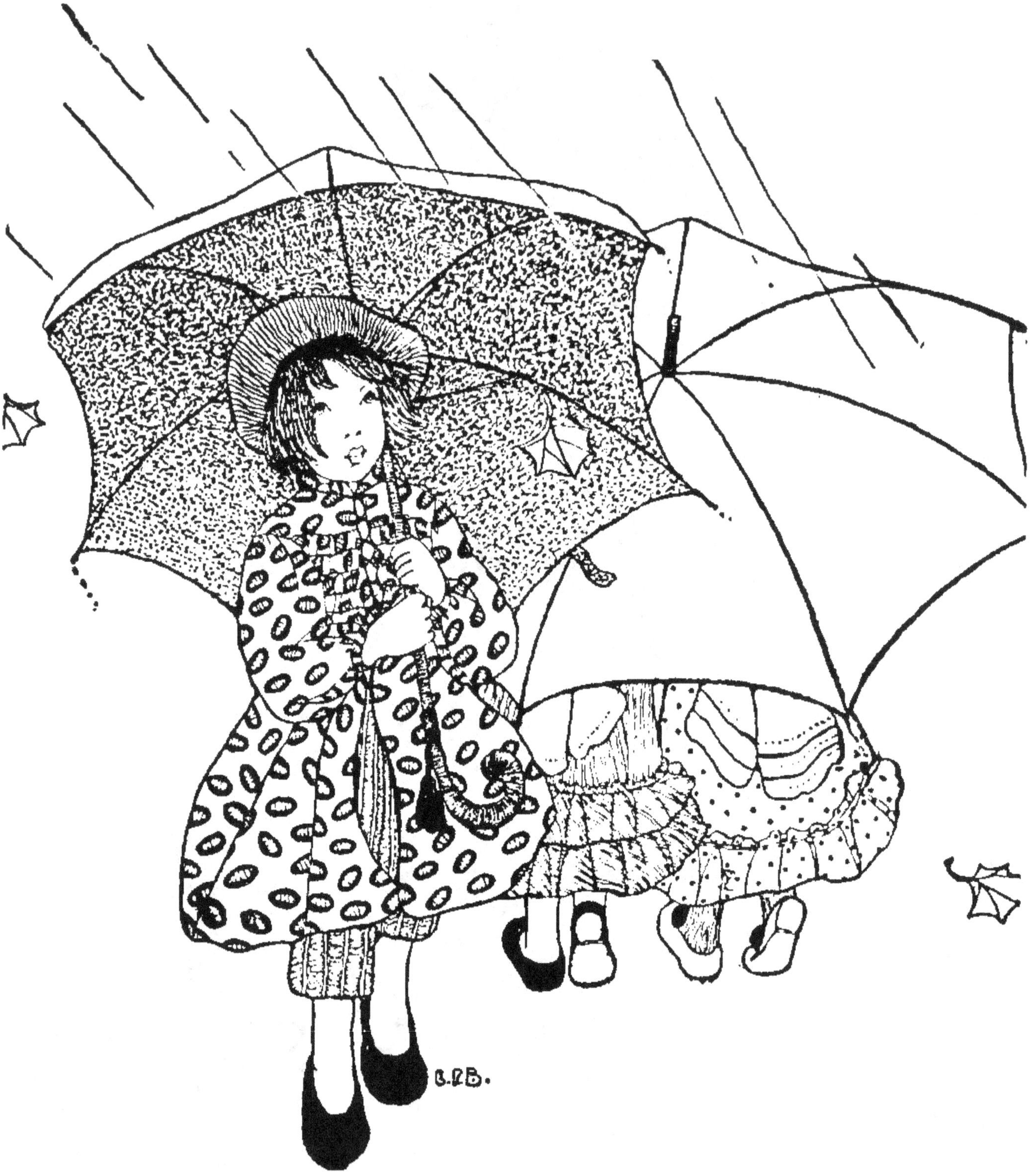
B.R.B.

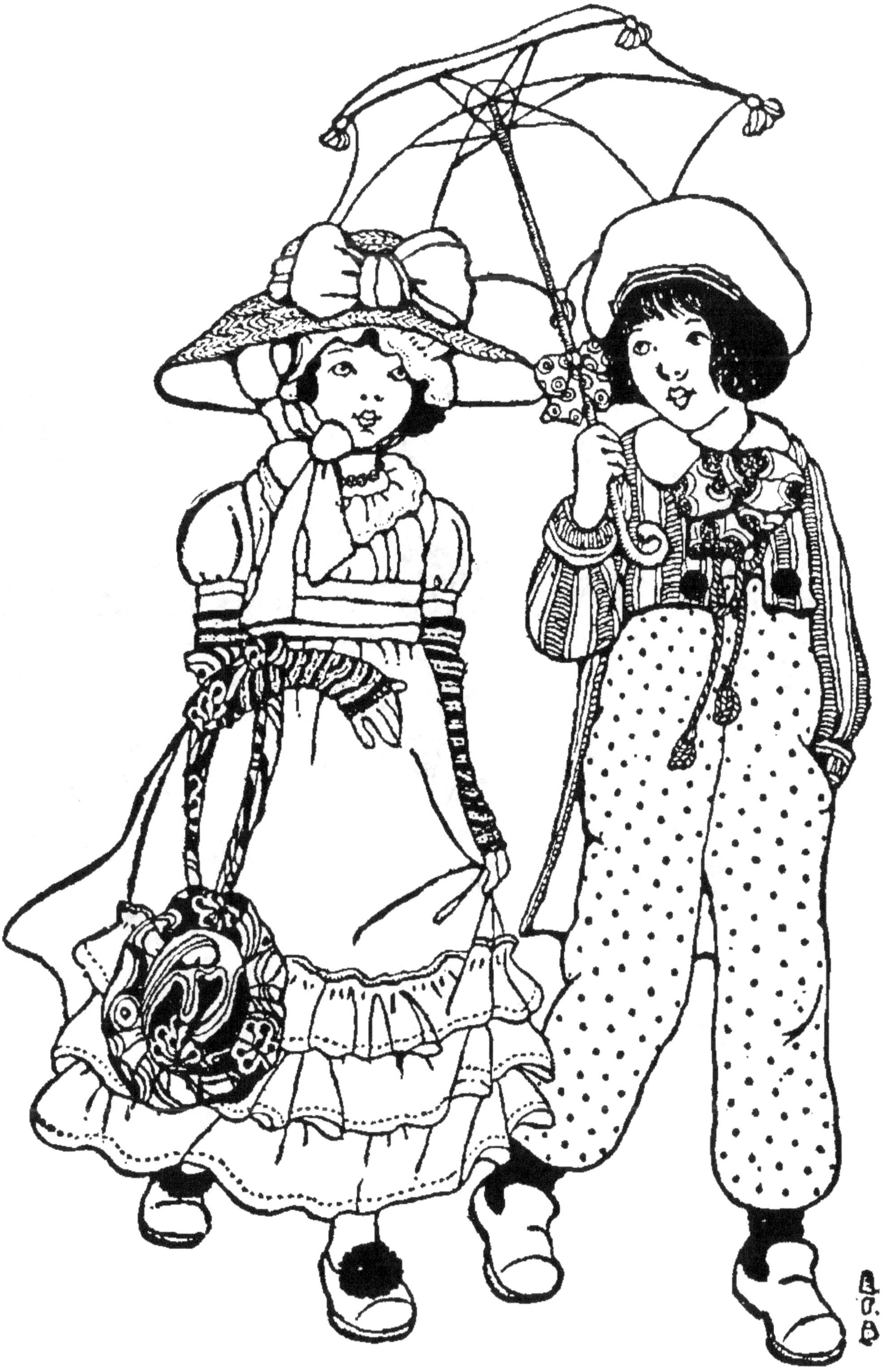

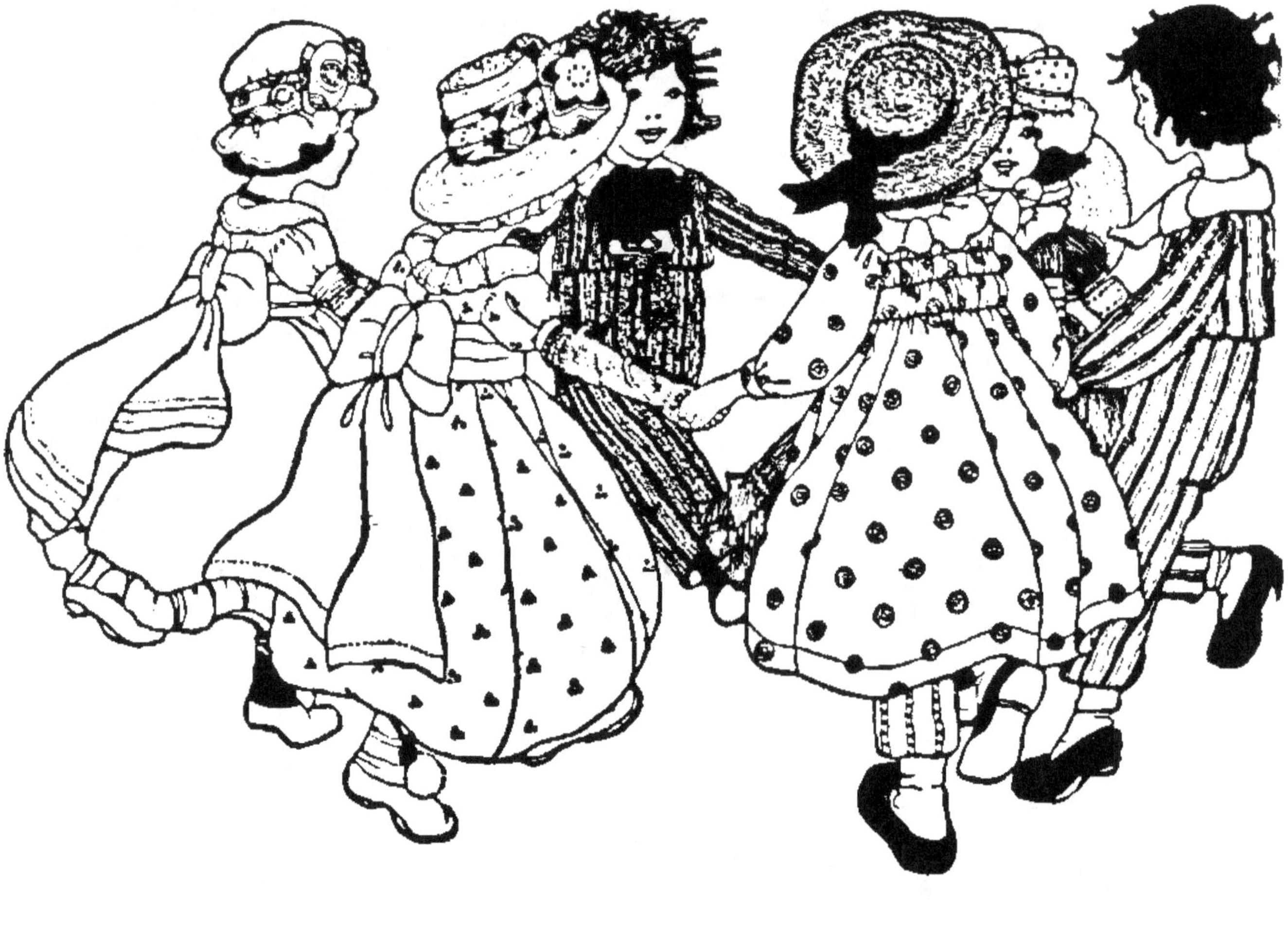

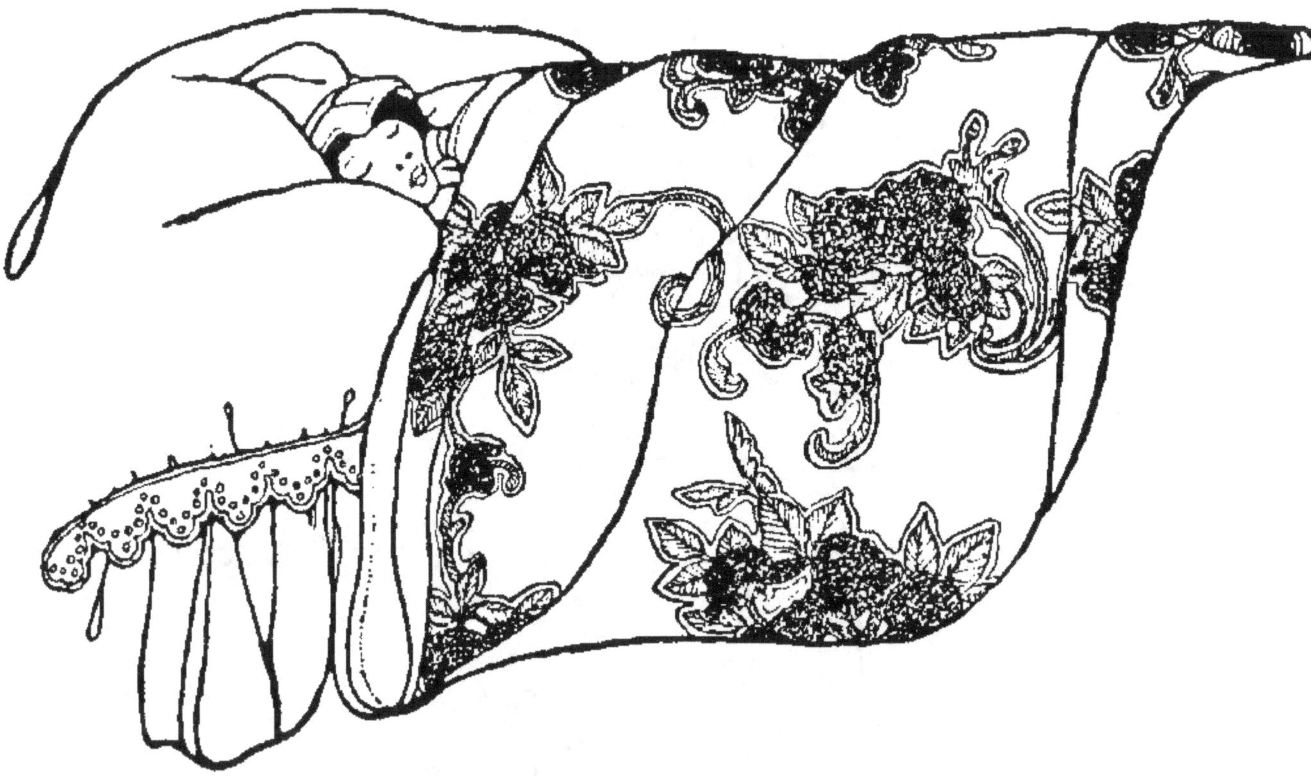

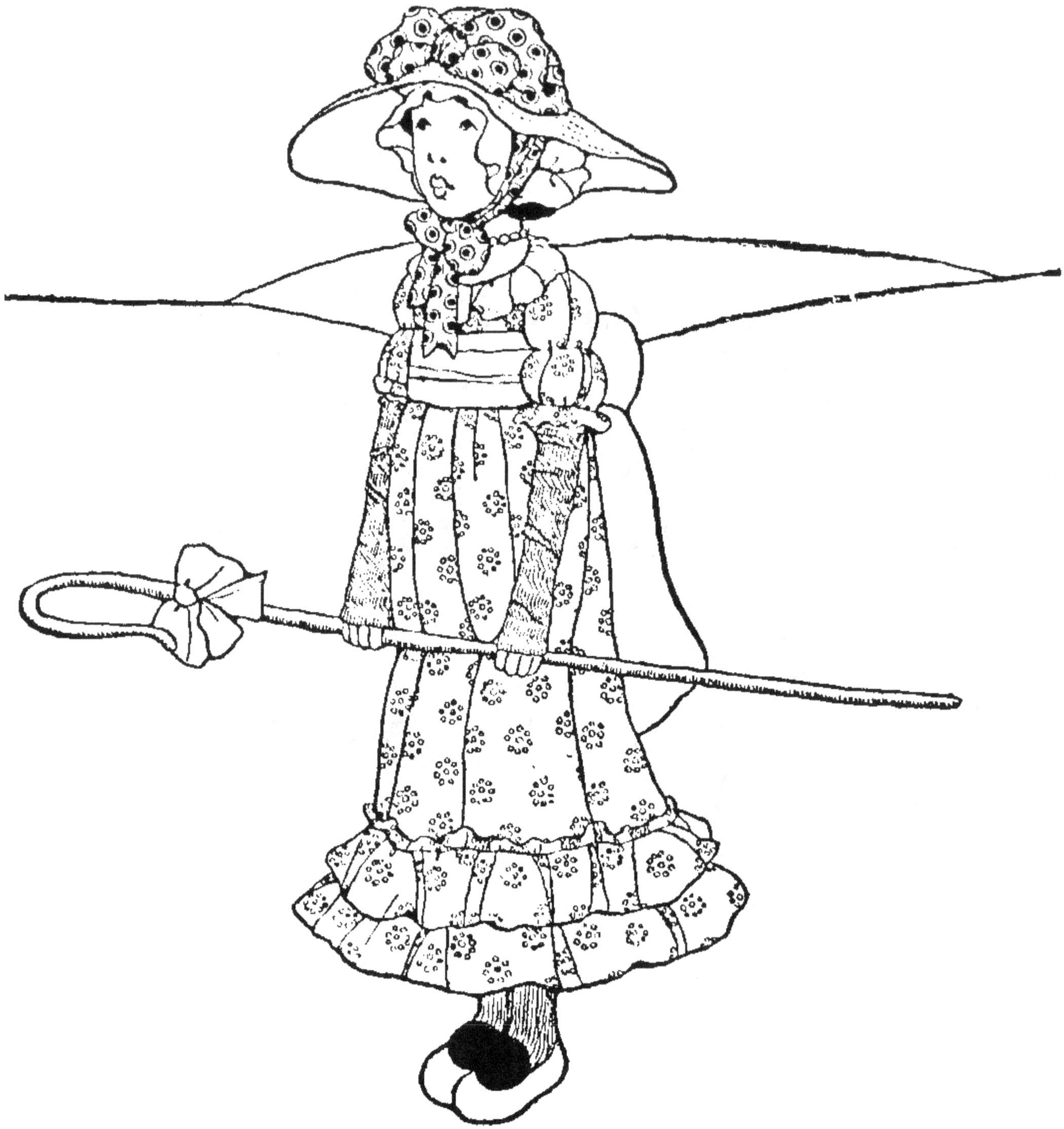

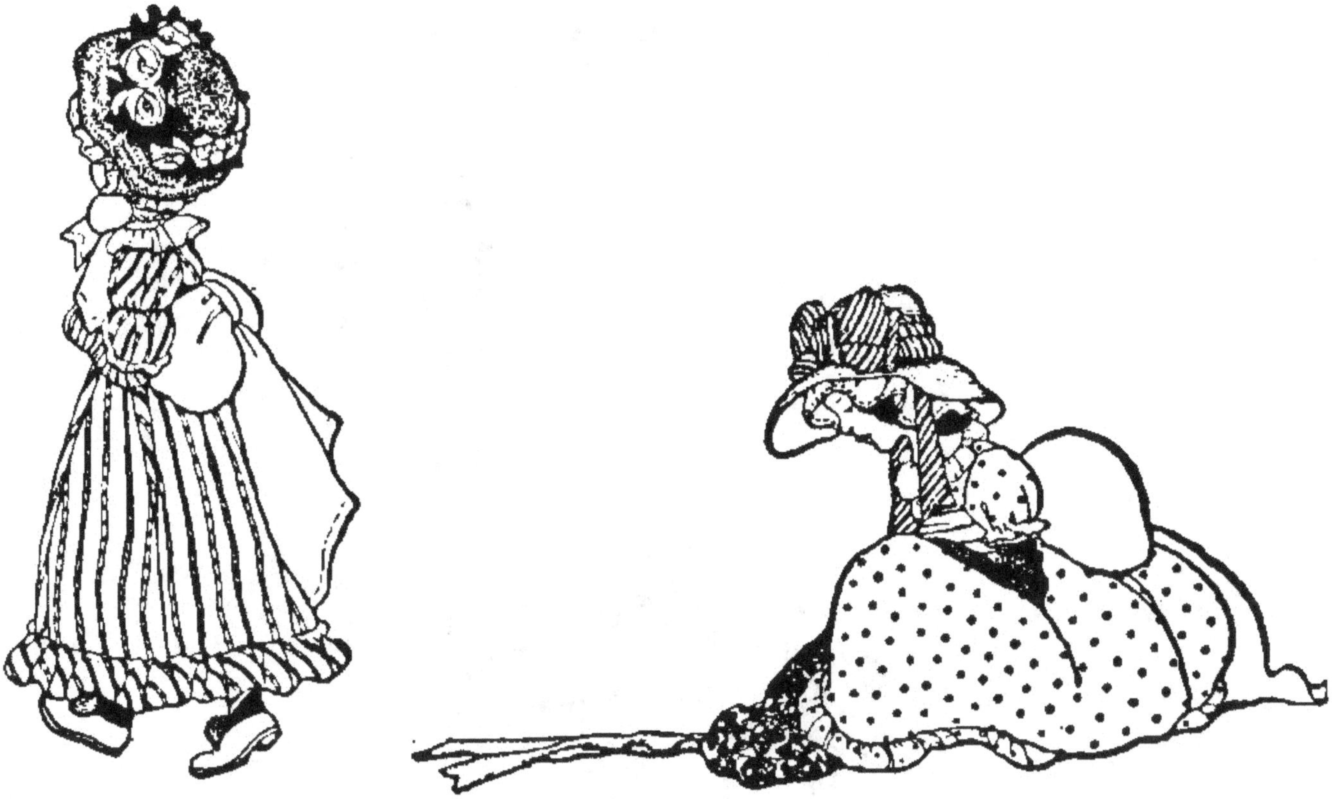

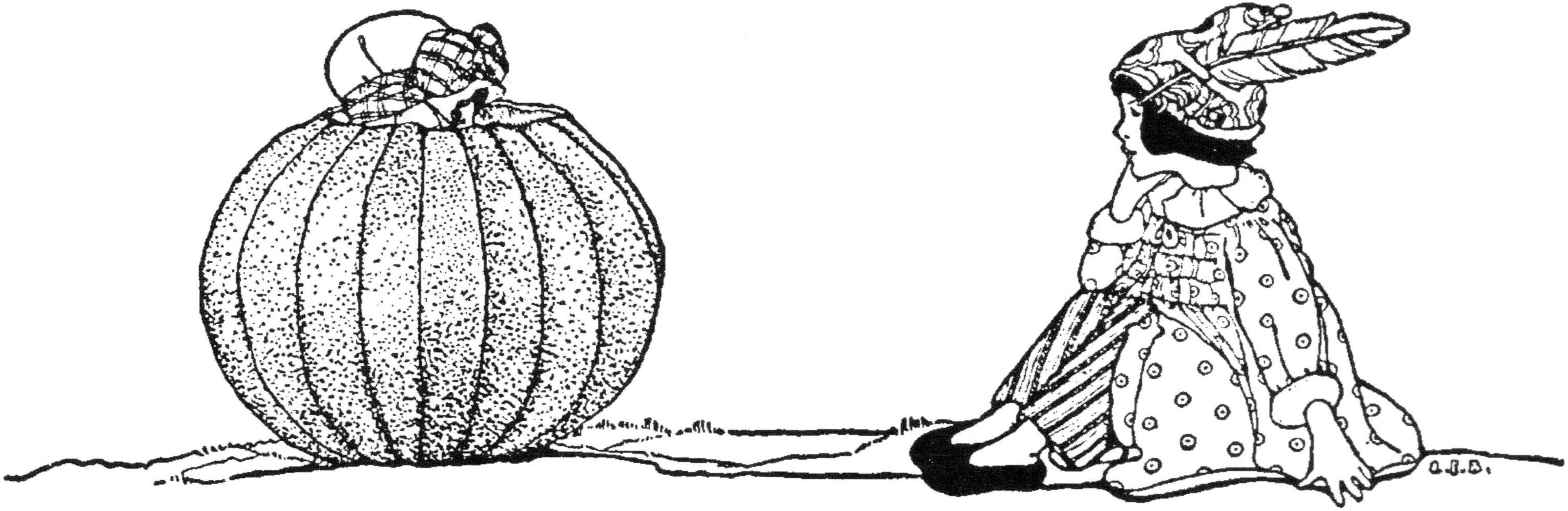

Peter, Peter, Pumpkin Eater.

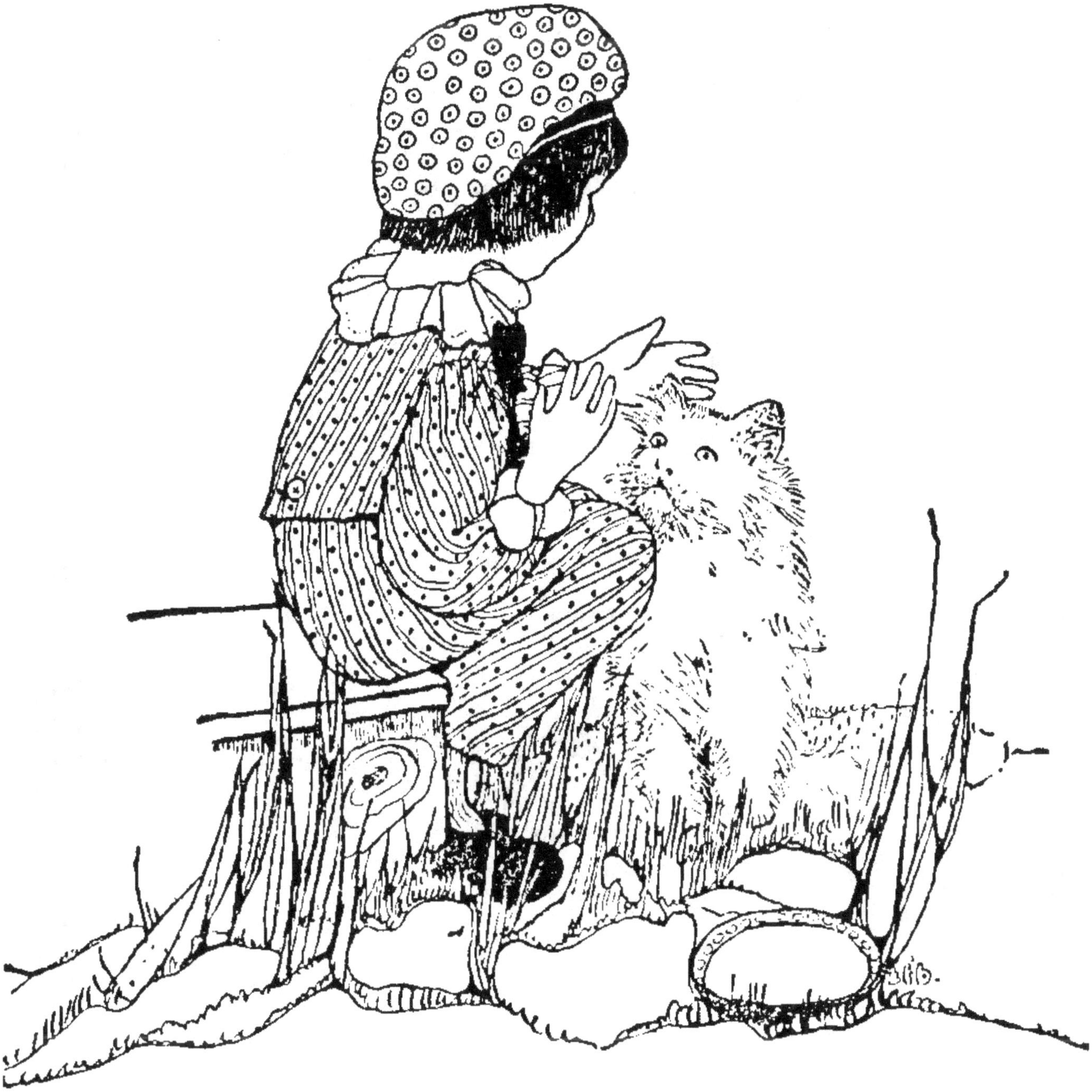

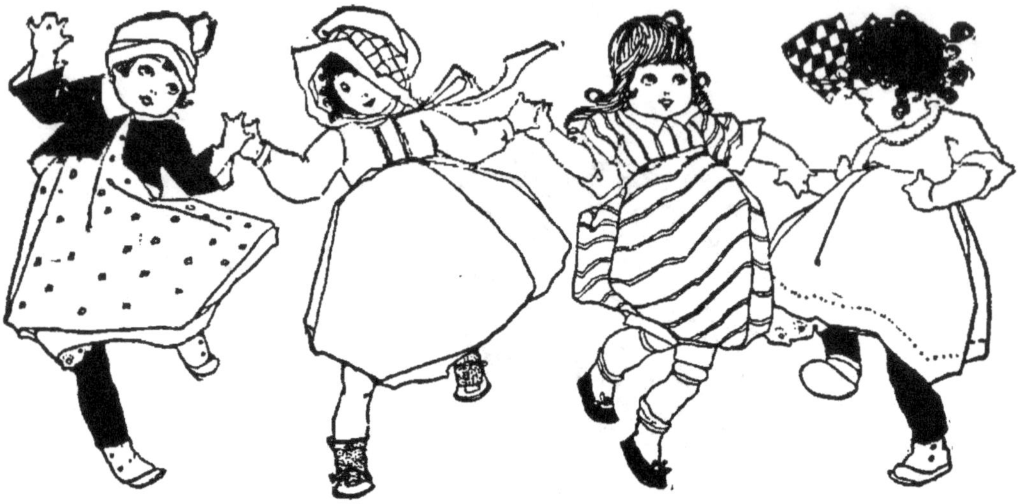

A HOST *of* CHILDREN

Illustrations by
ETHEL FRANKLIN BETTS

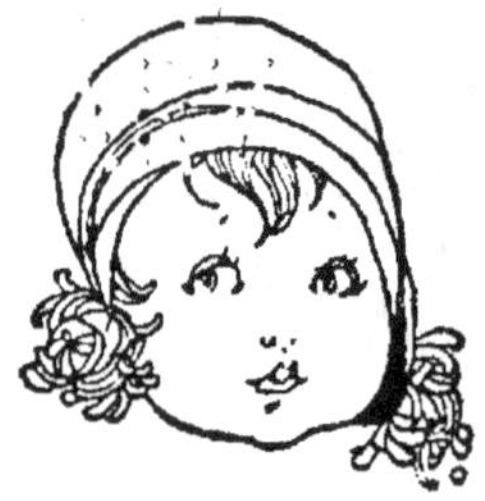

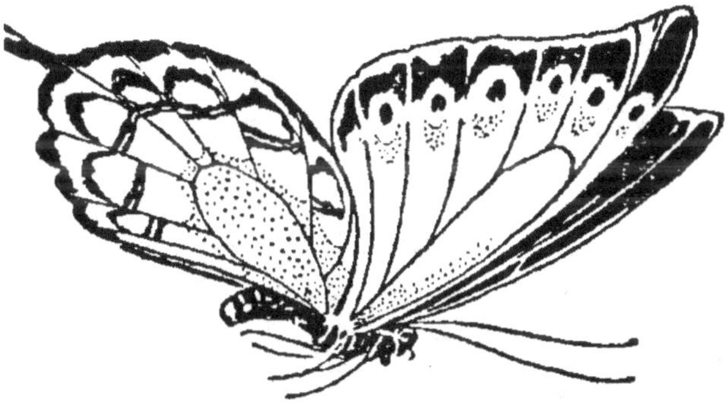

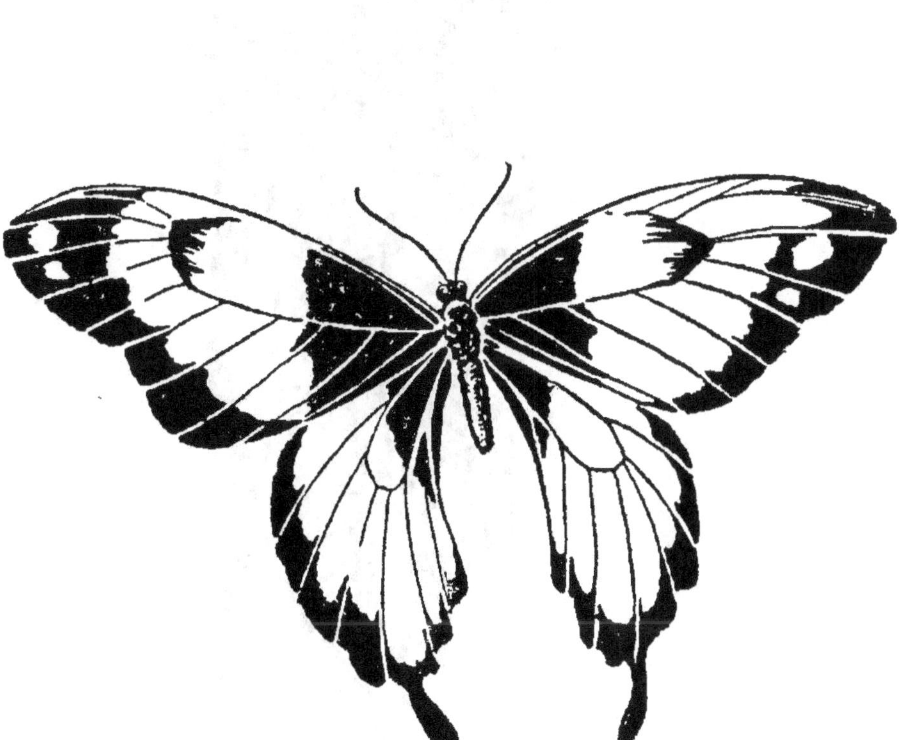

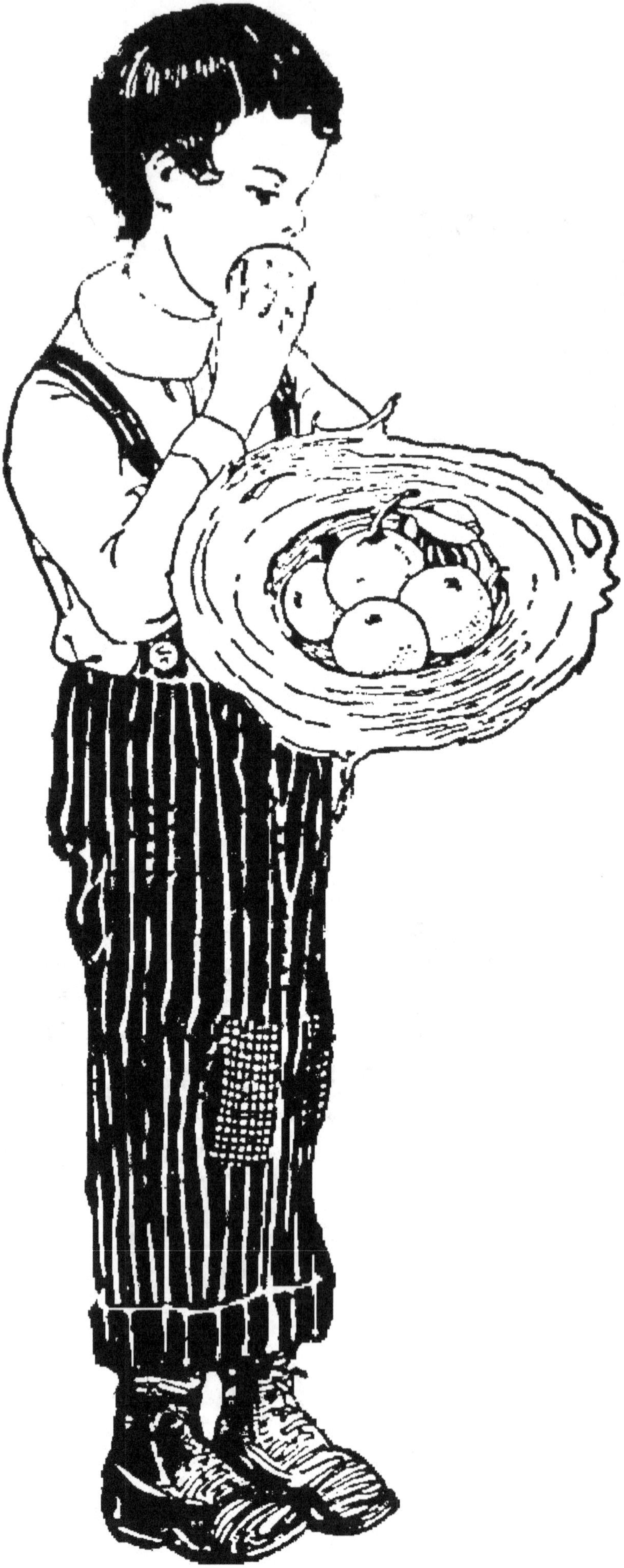

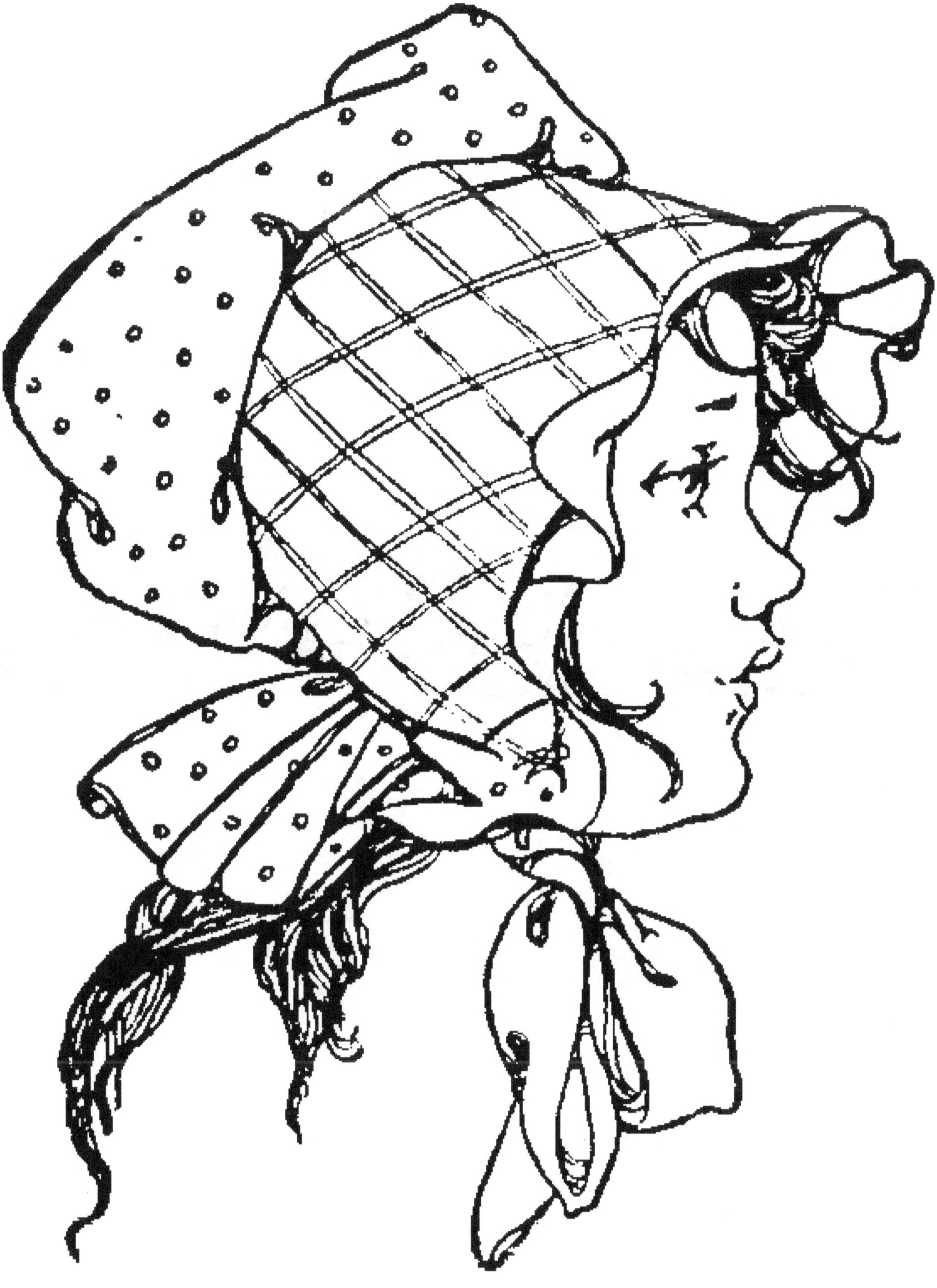

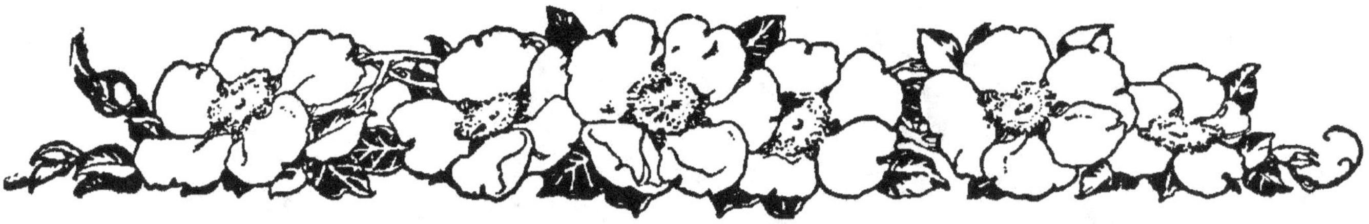

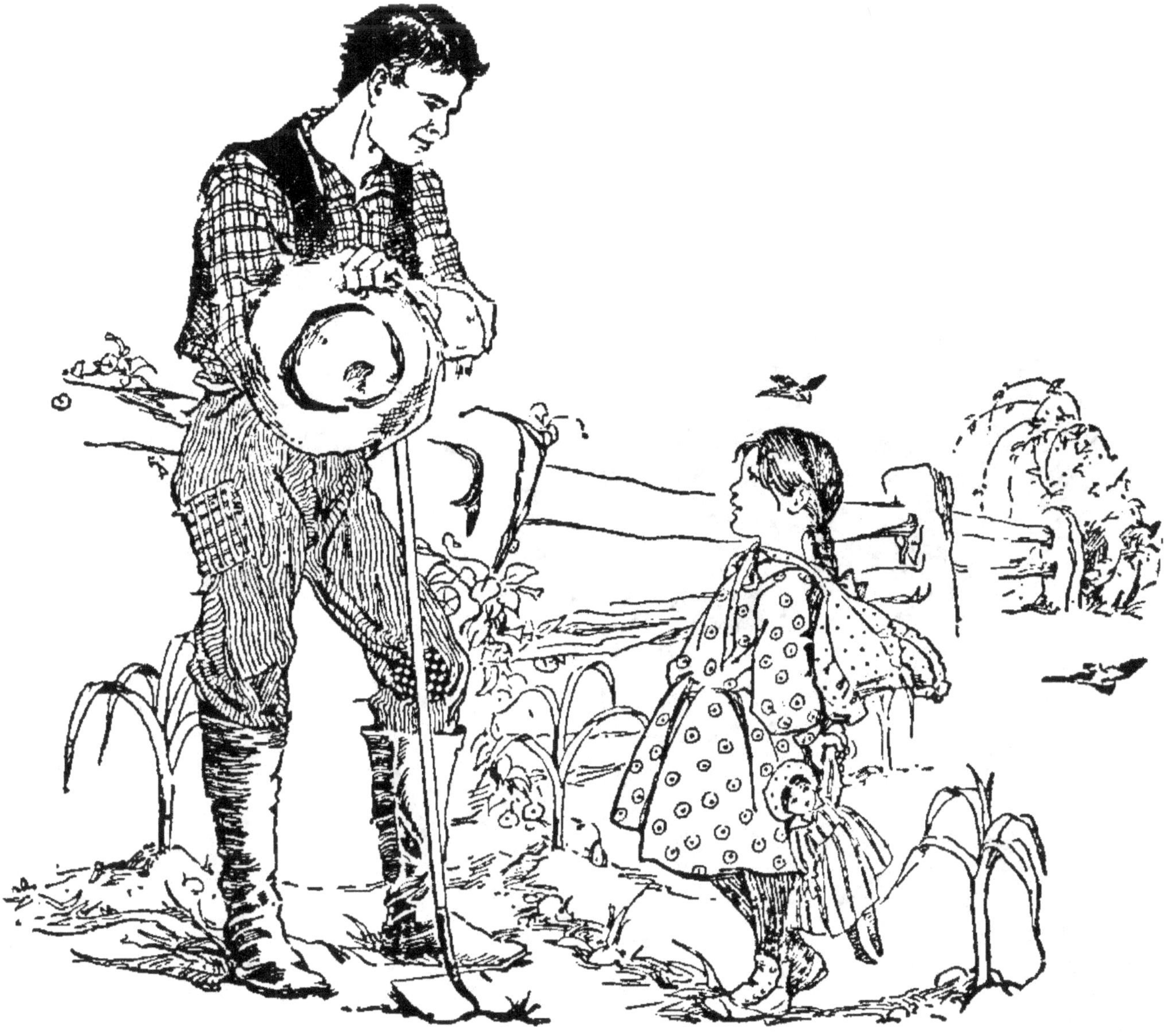

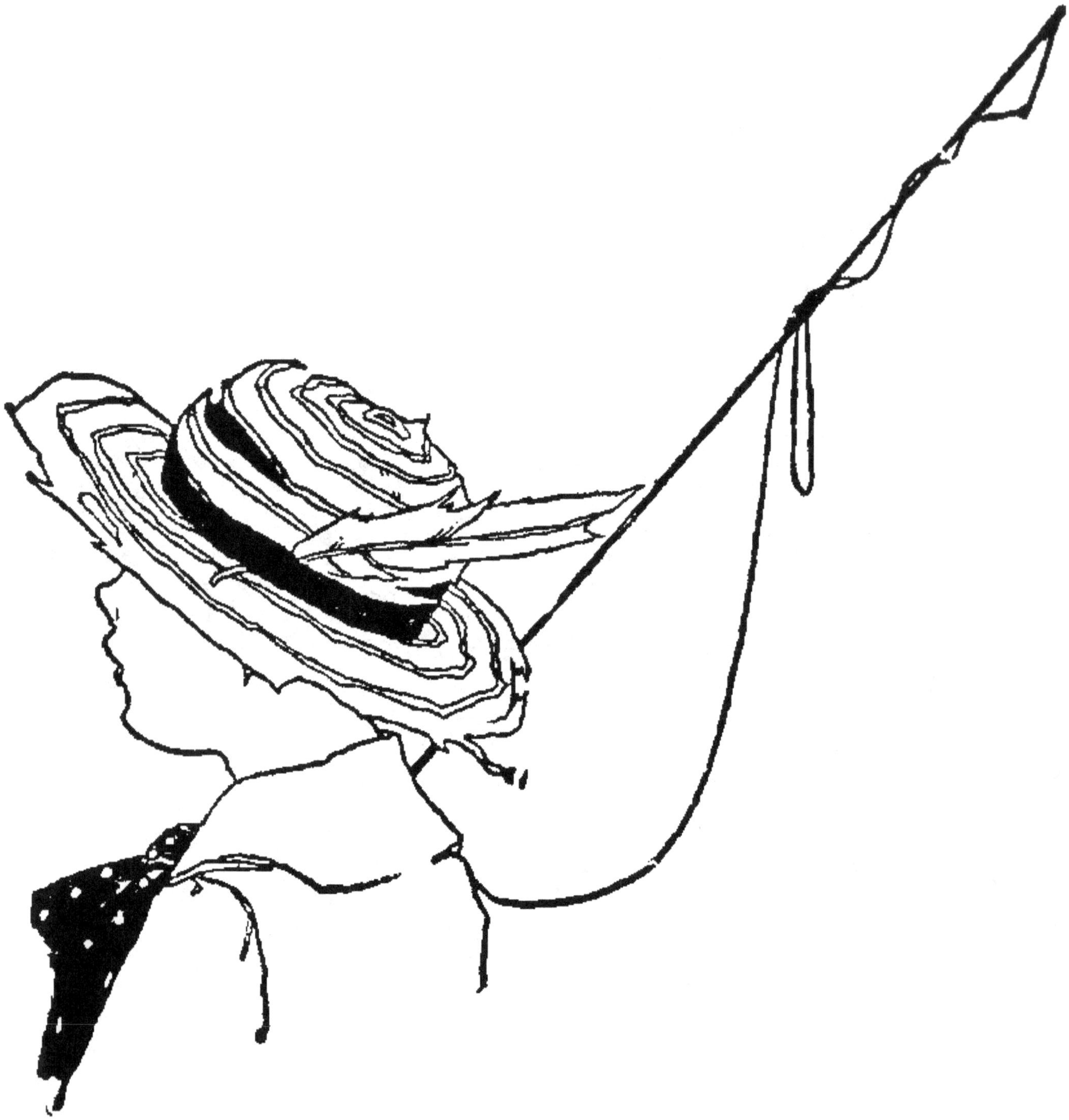

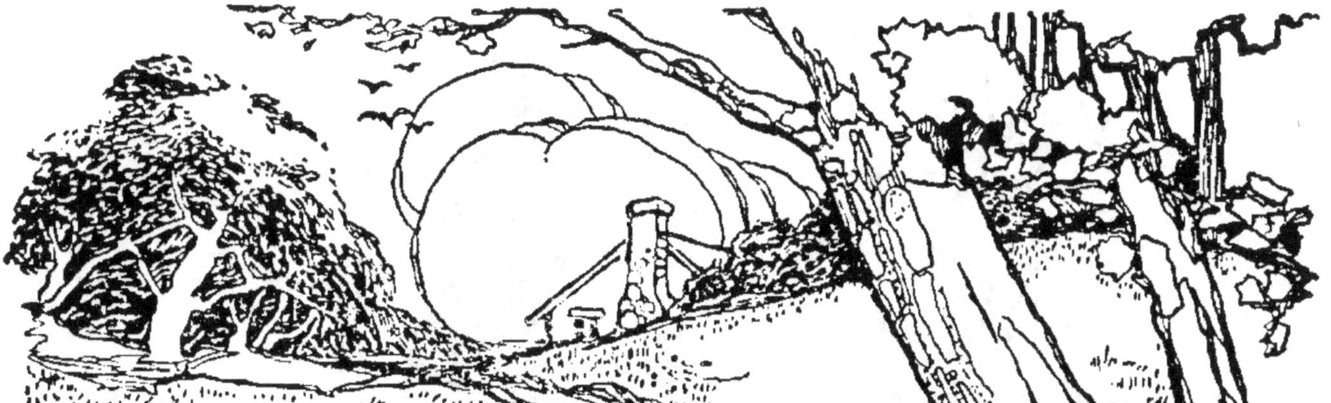

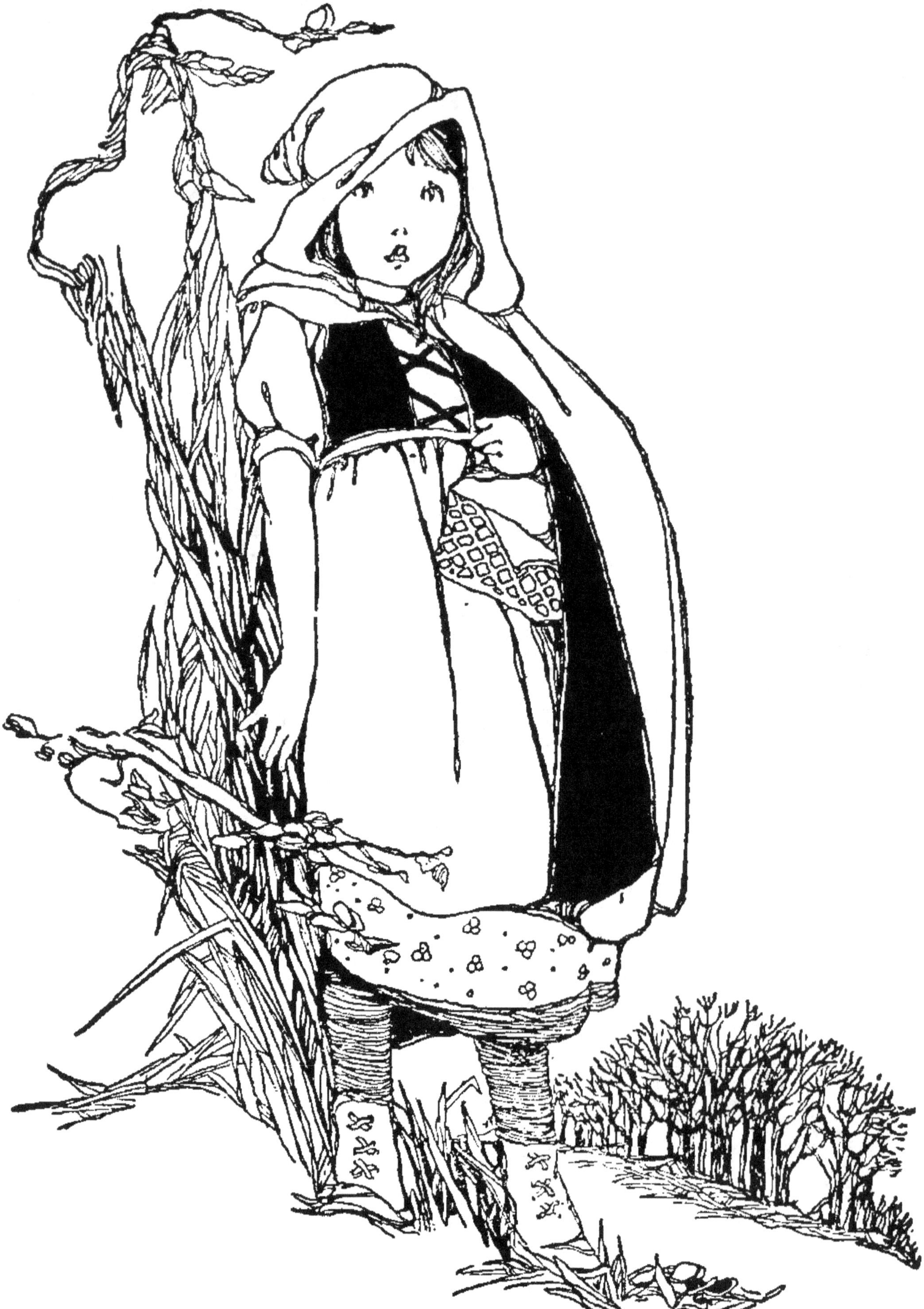

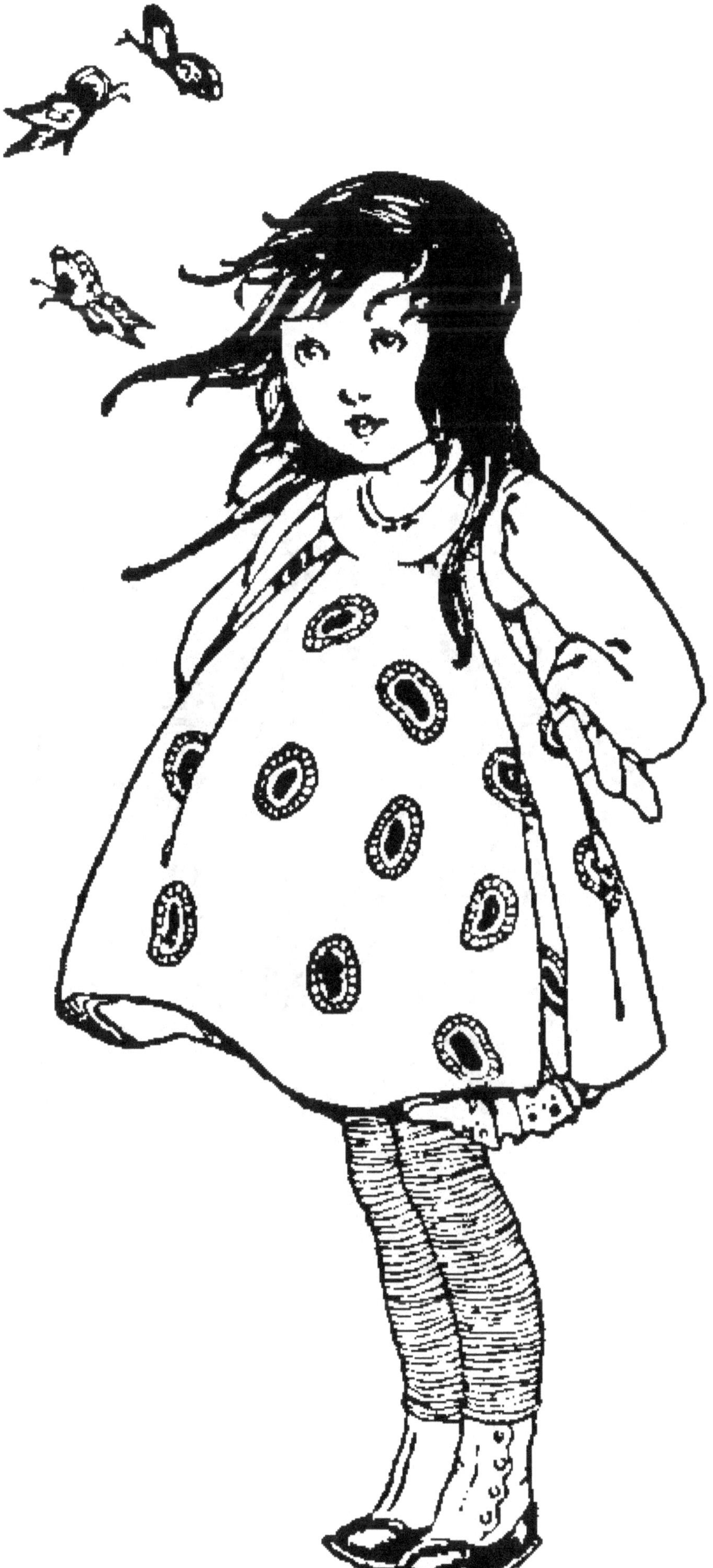

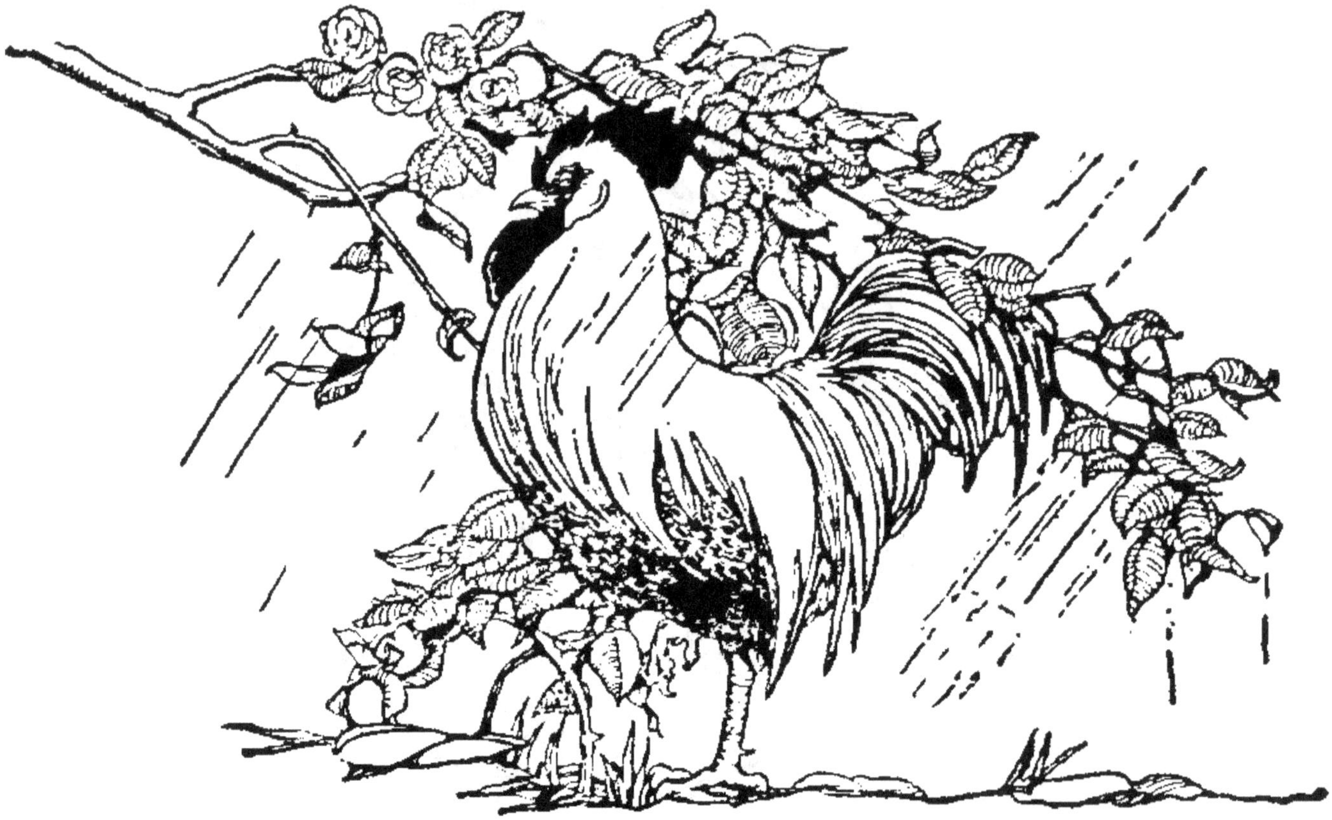

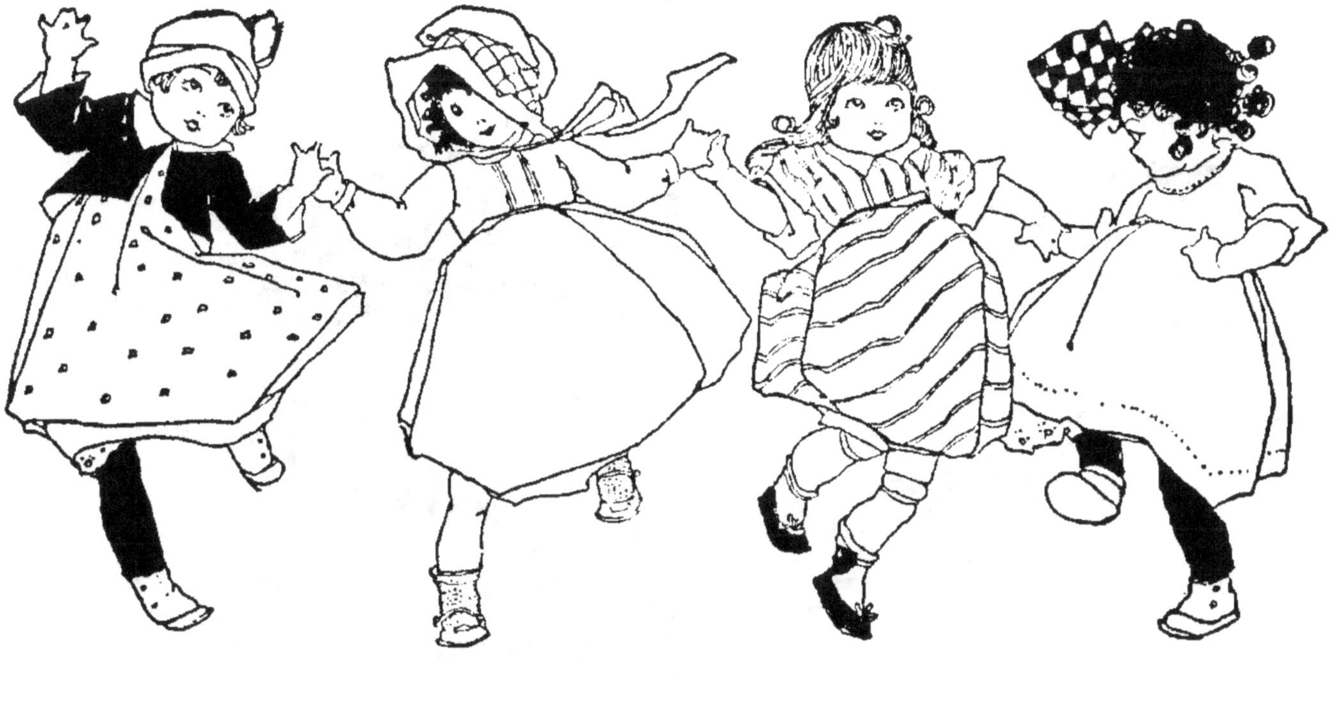

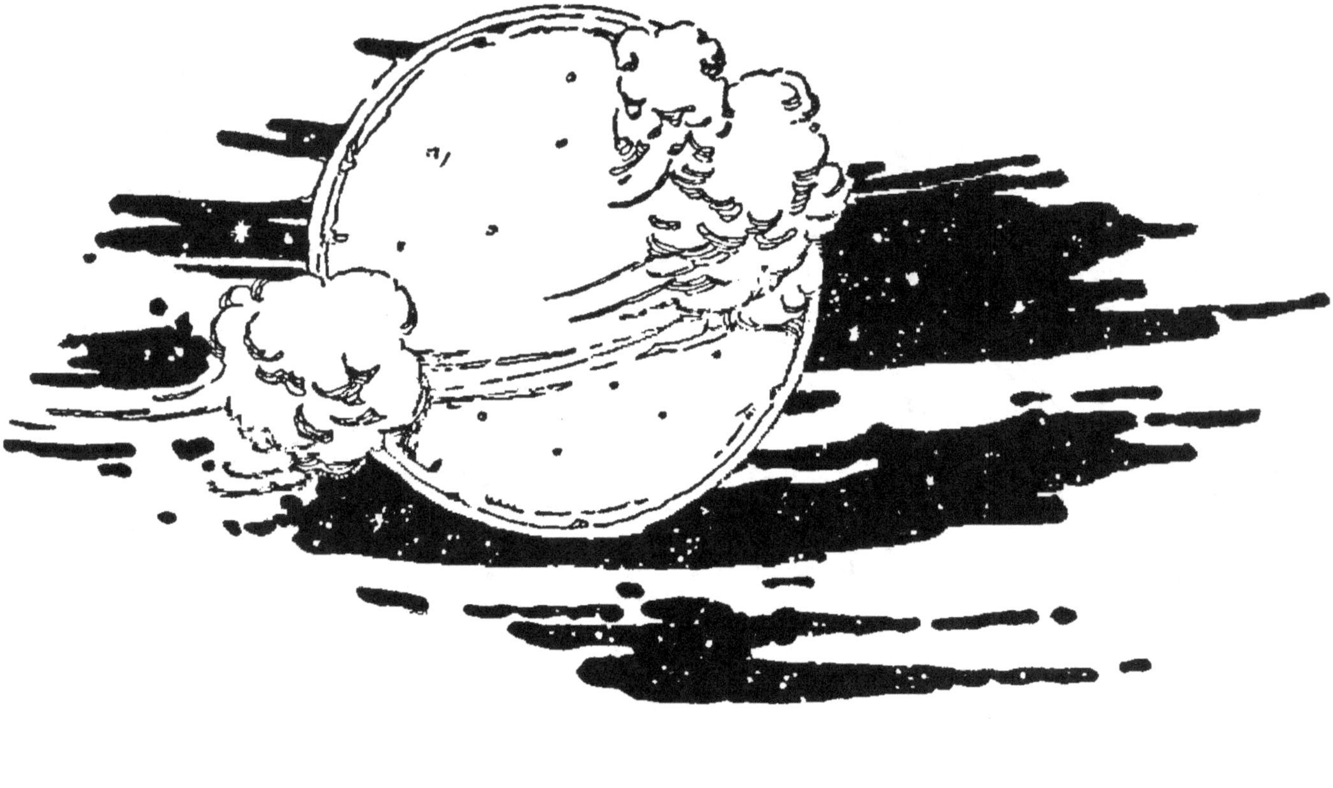

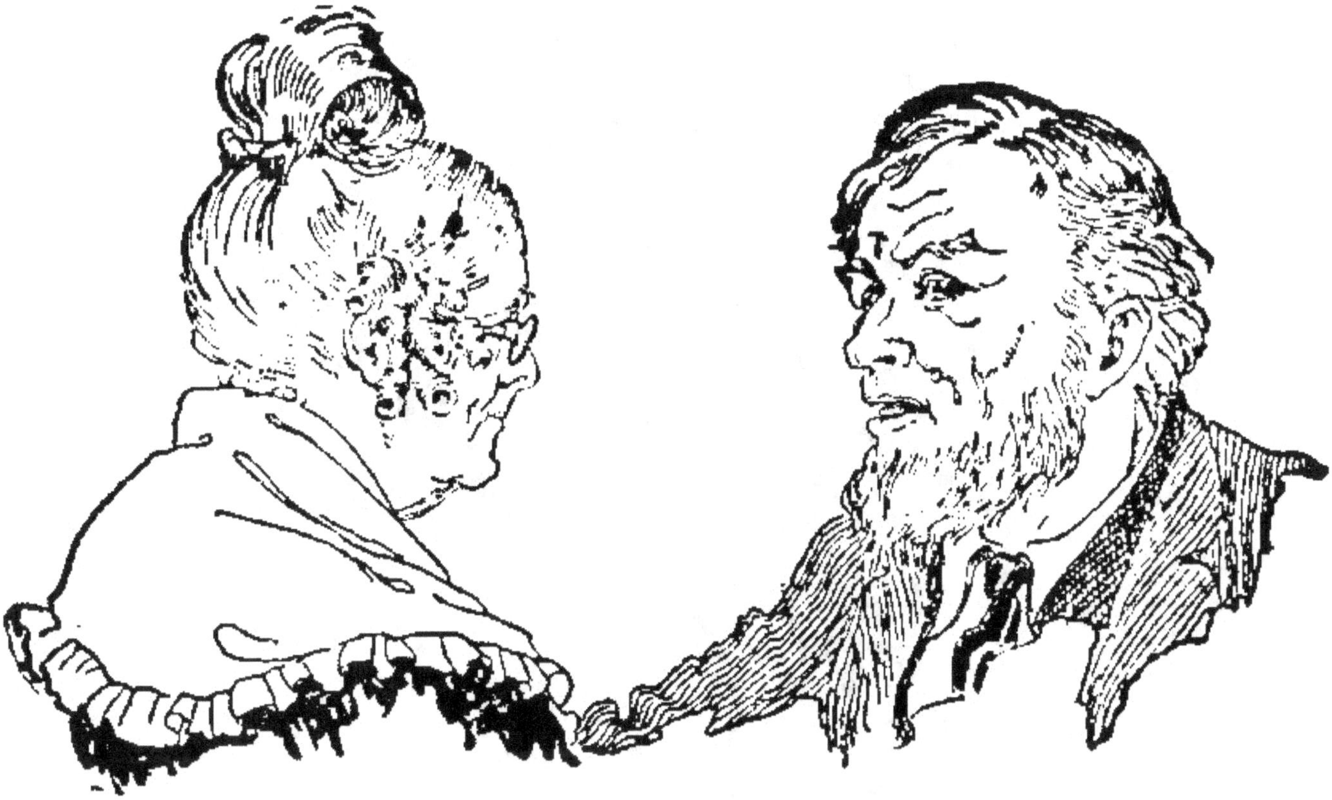

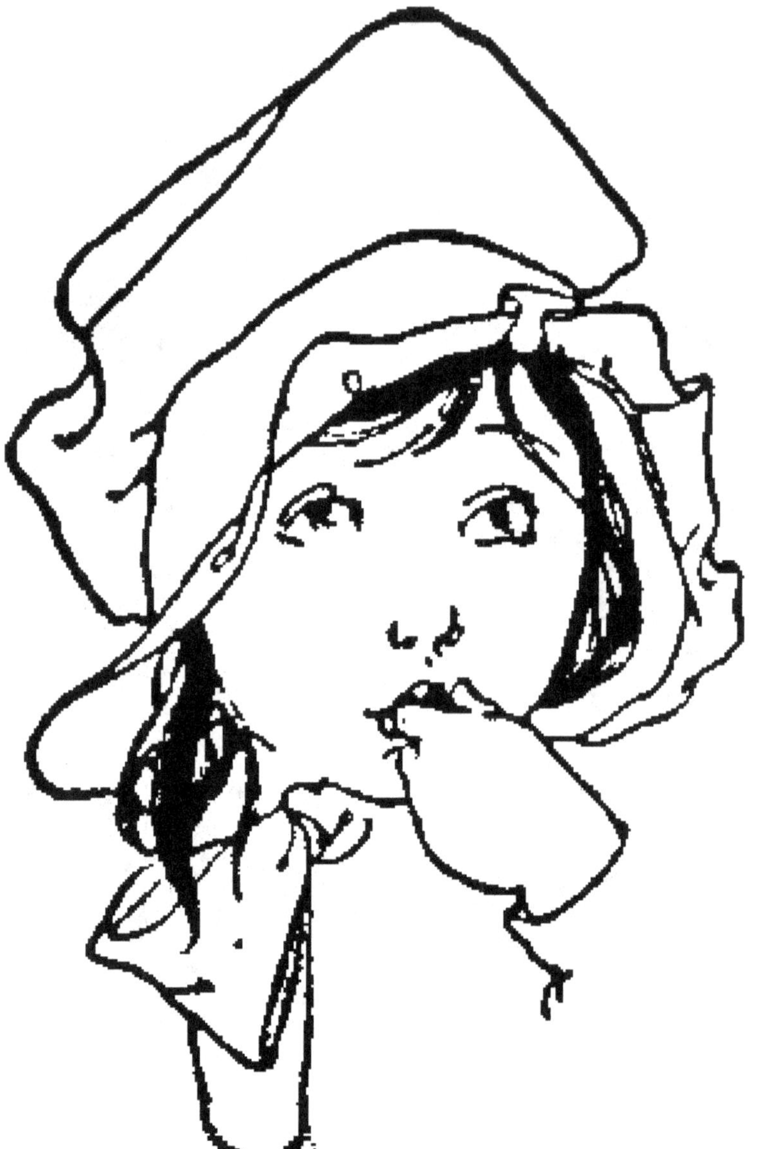

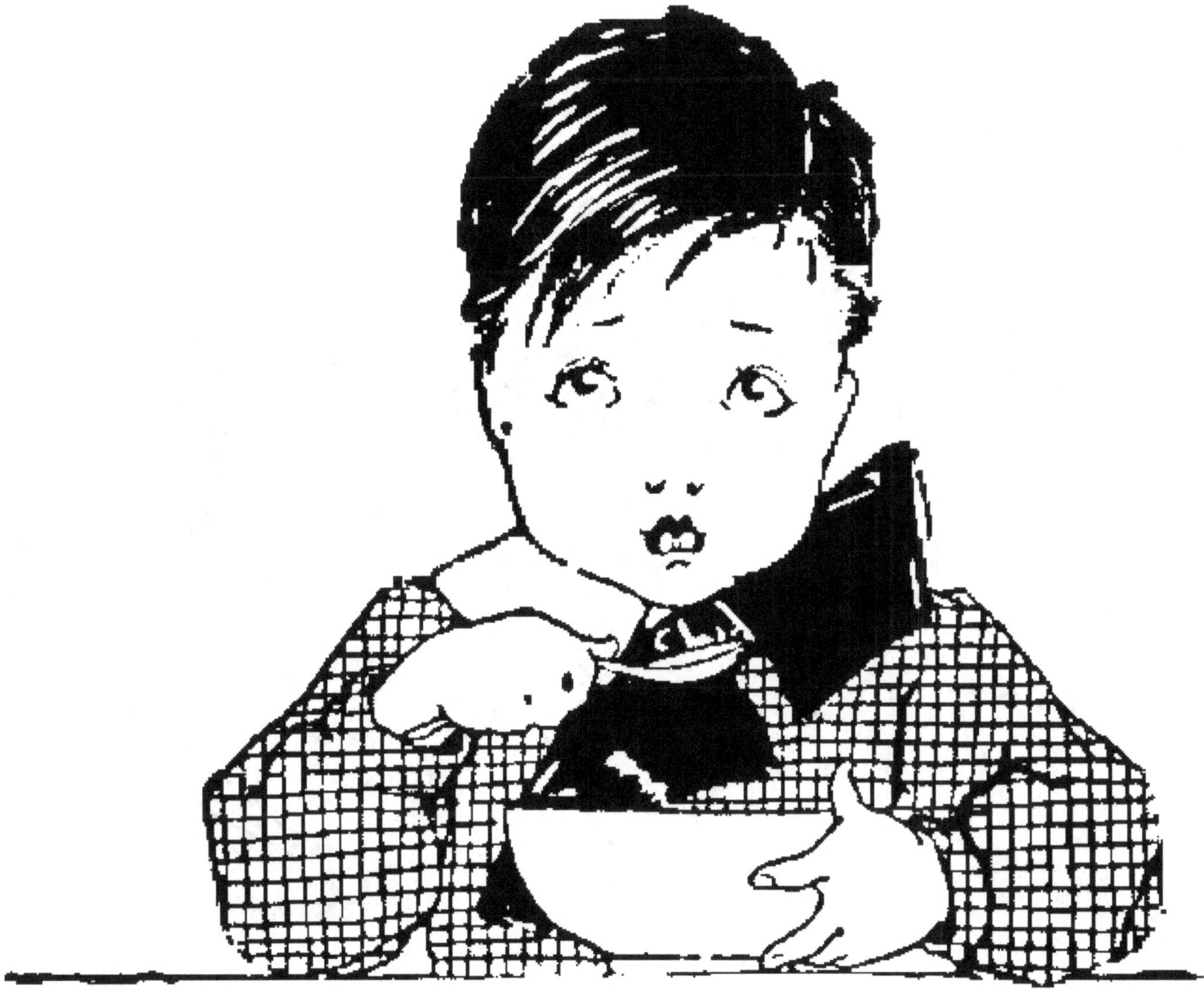

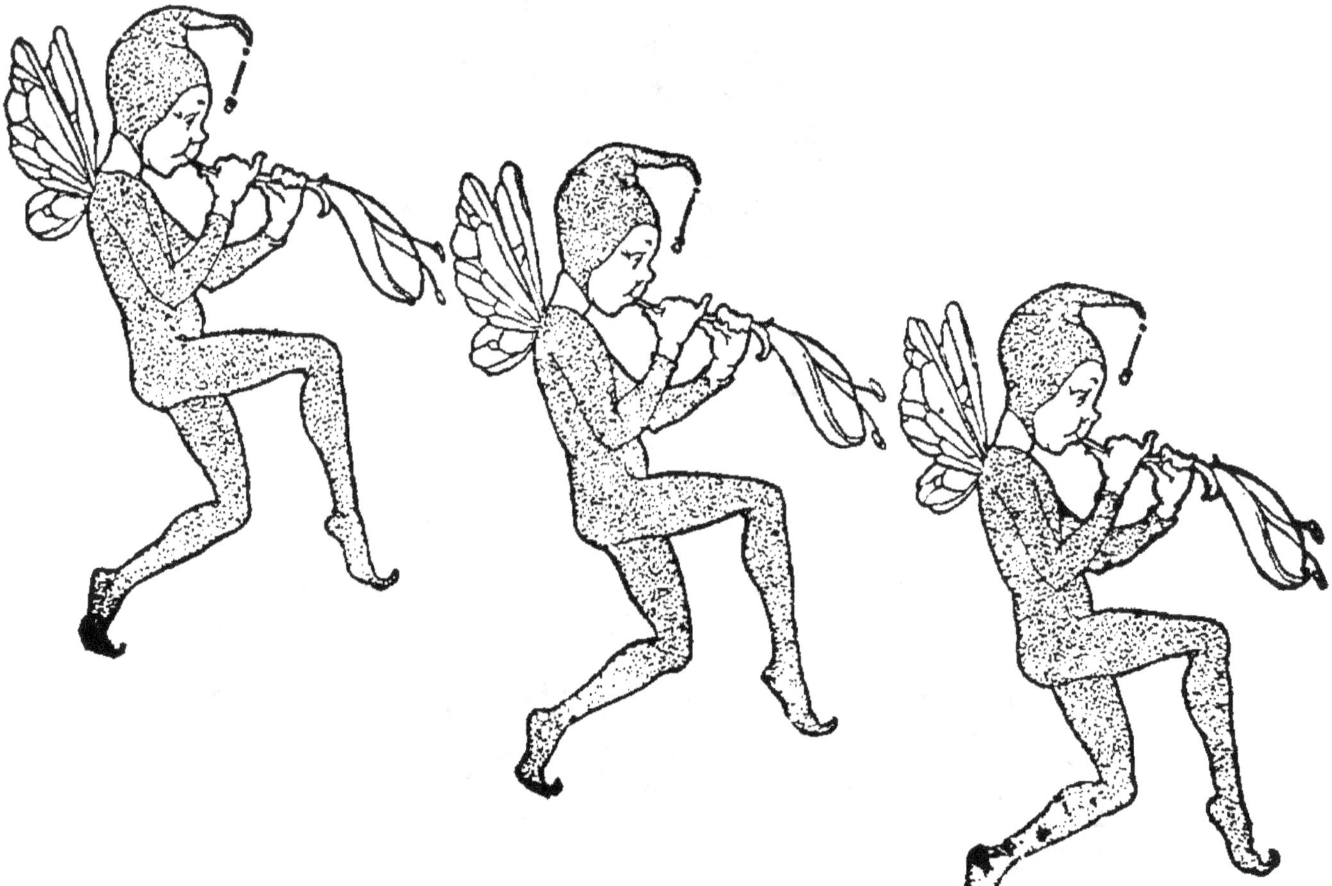

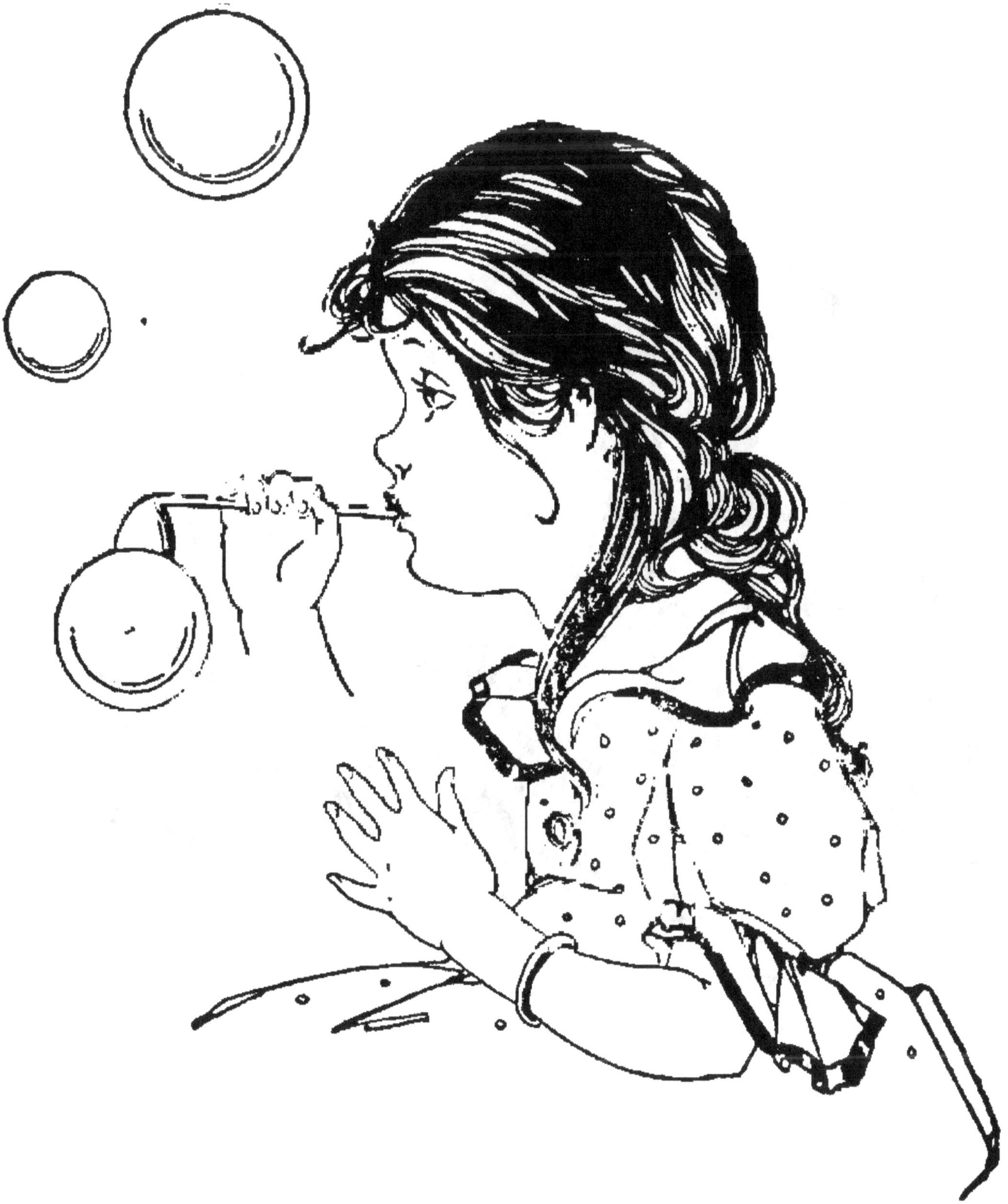

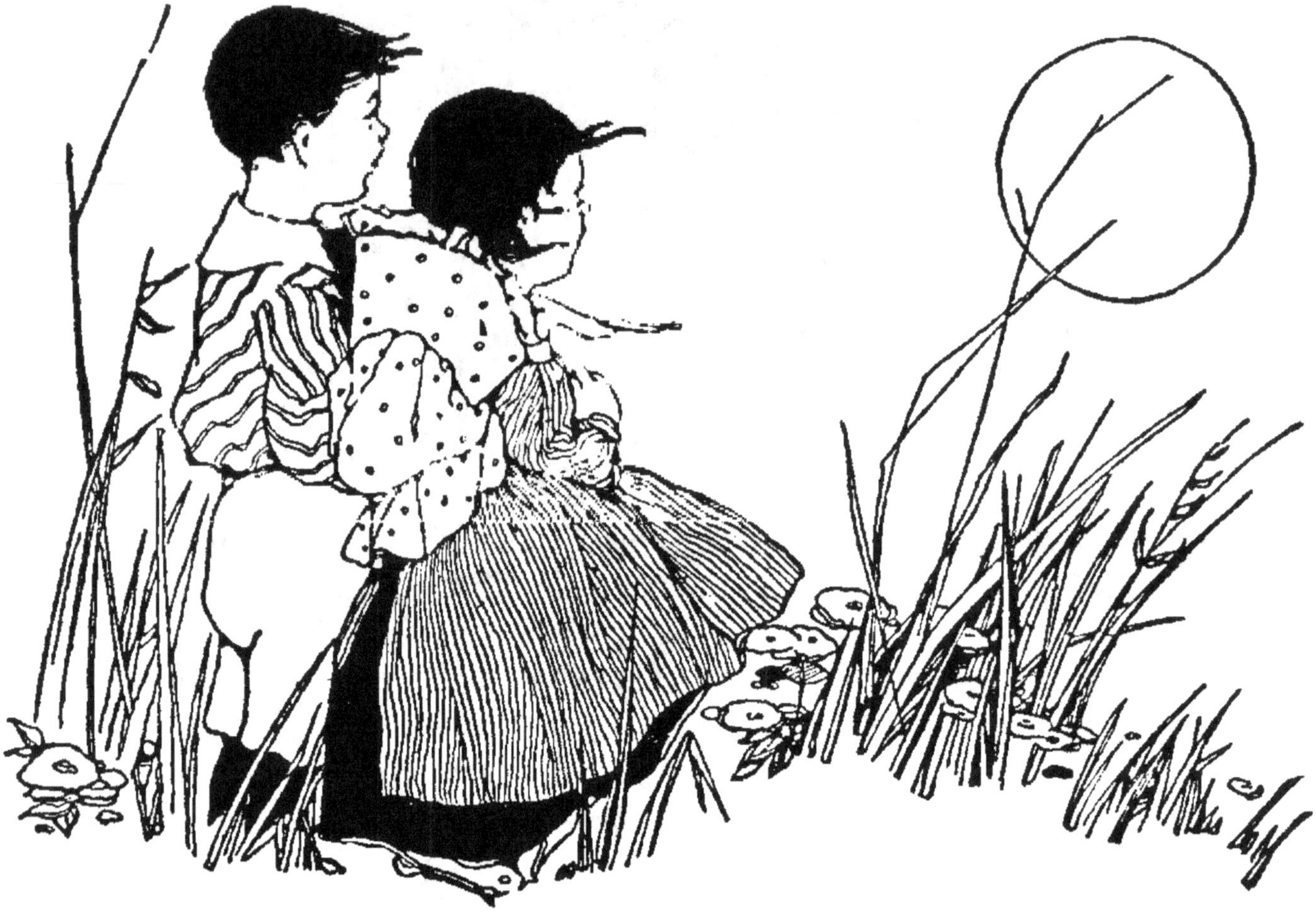

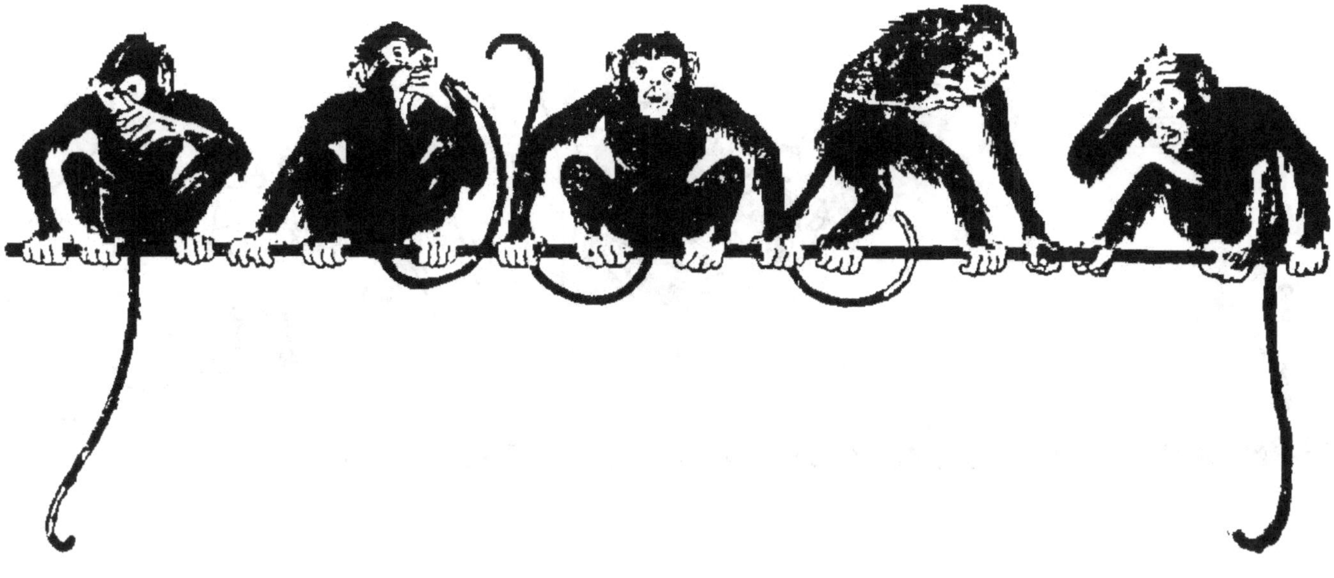

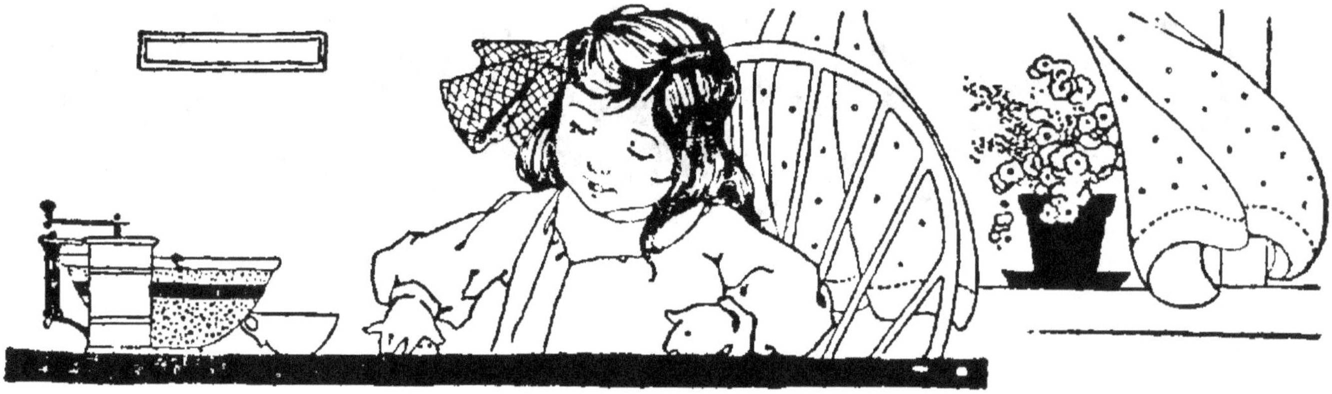

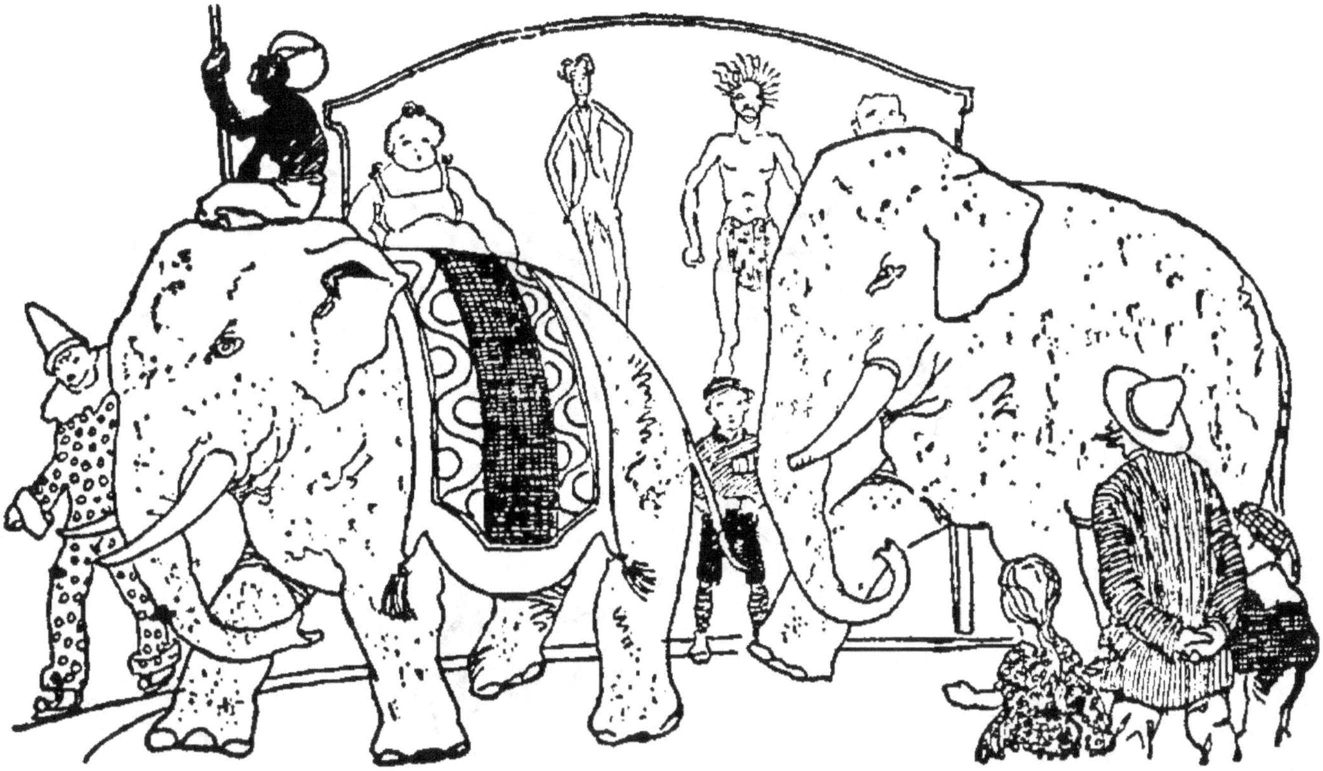

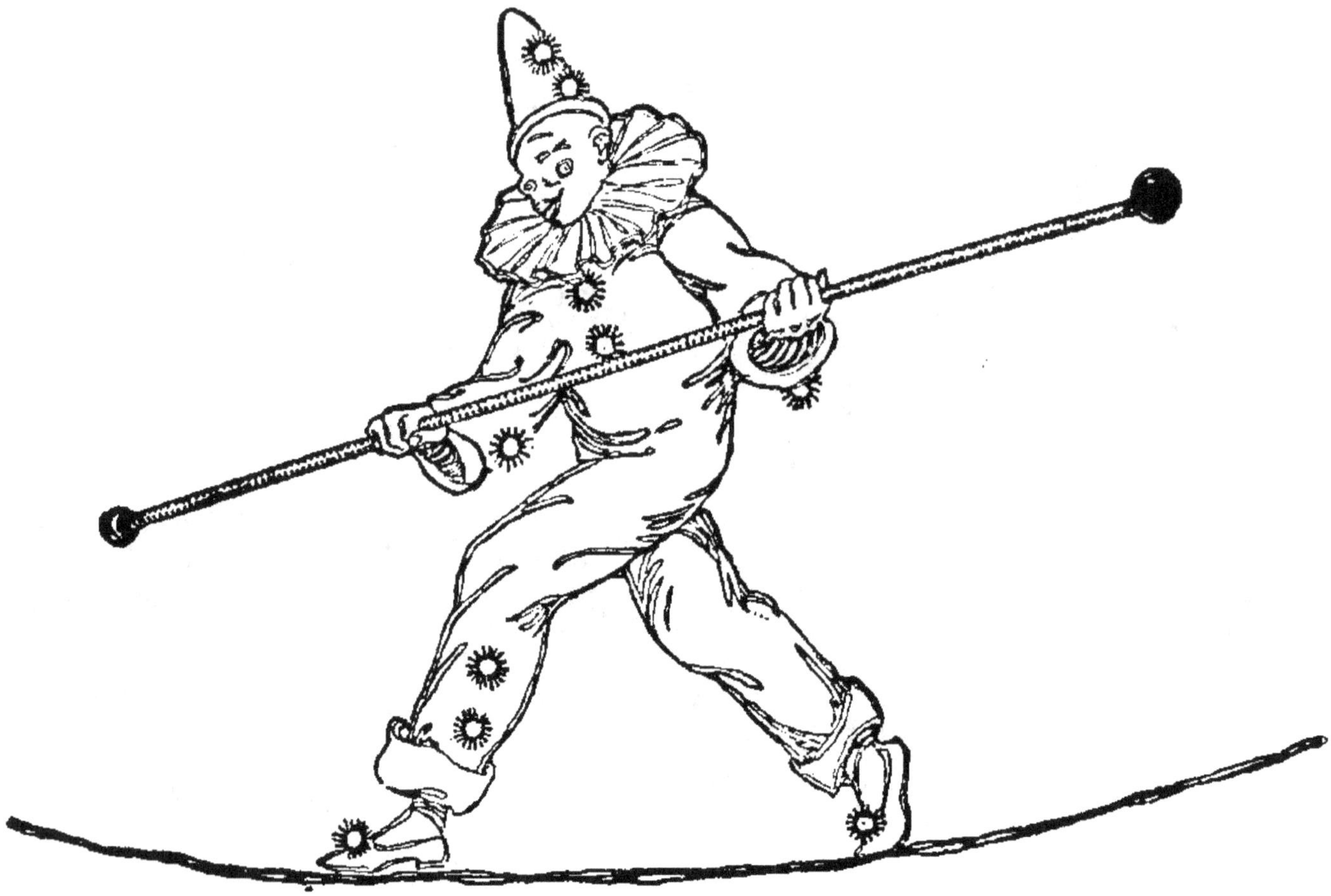

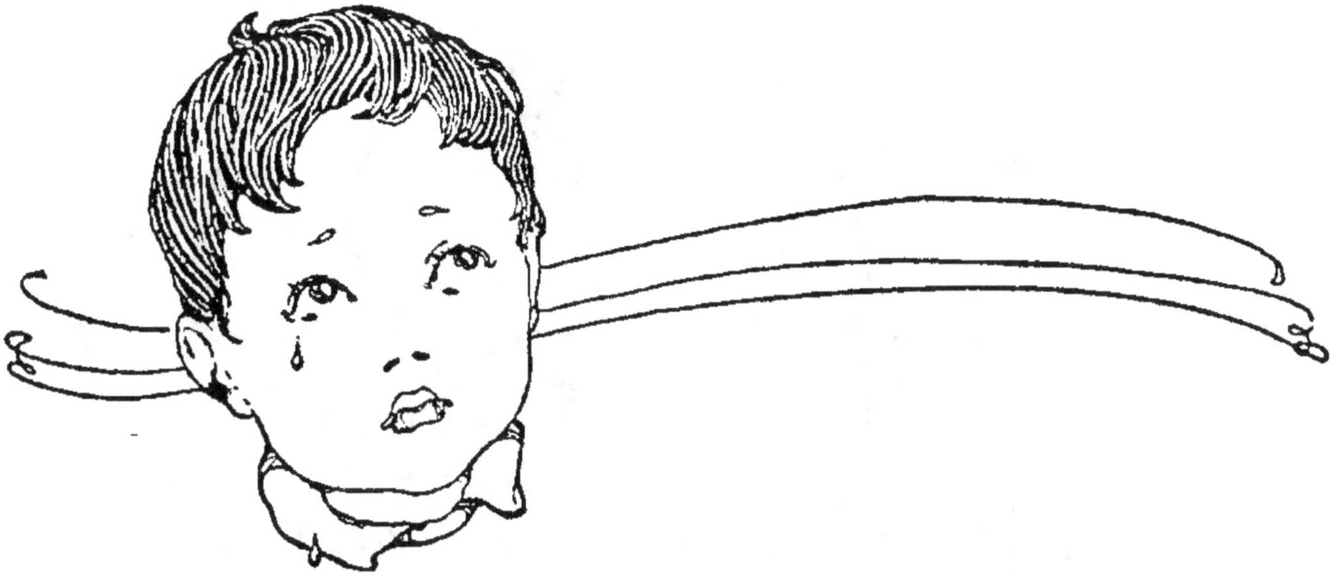

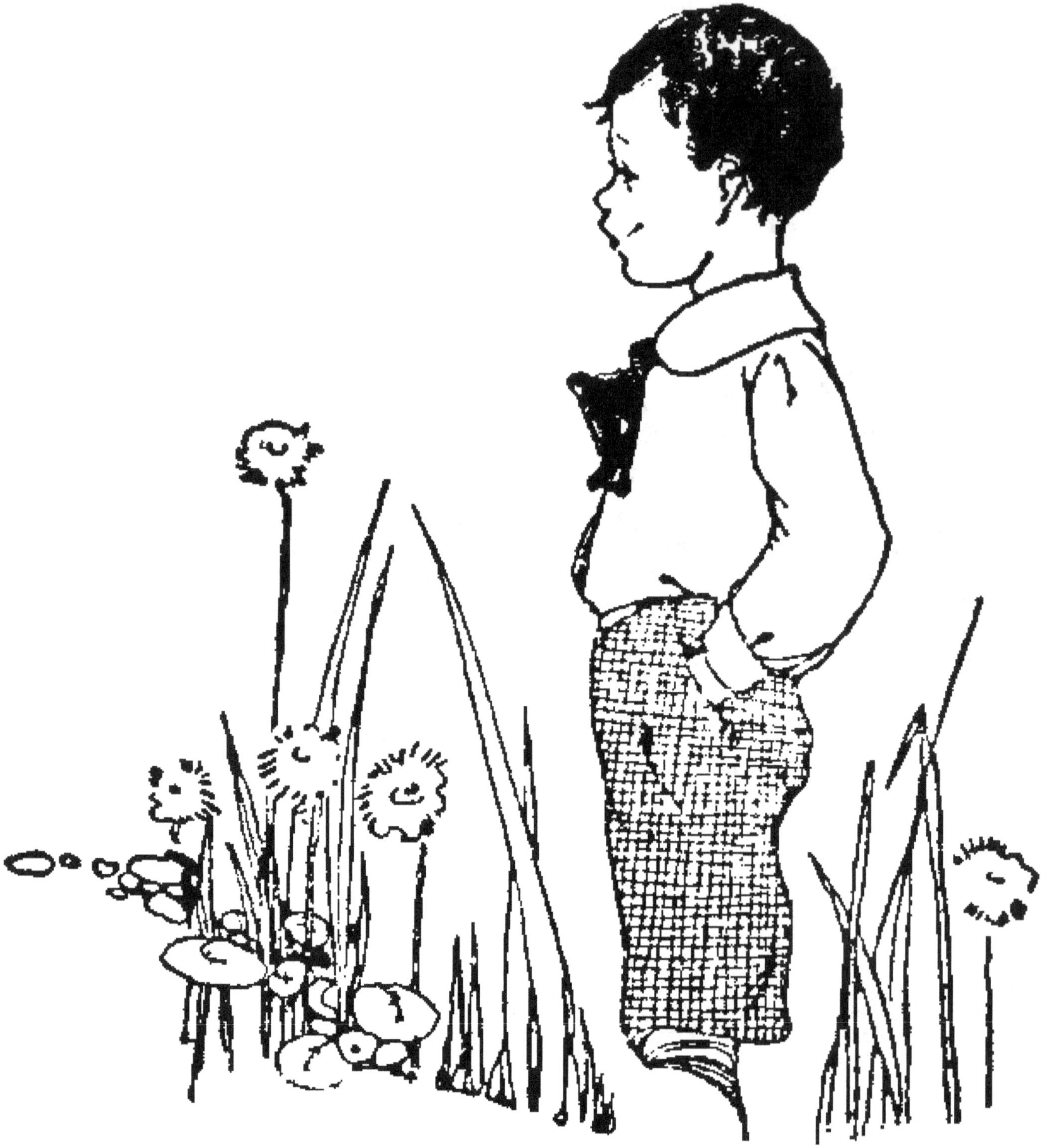

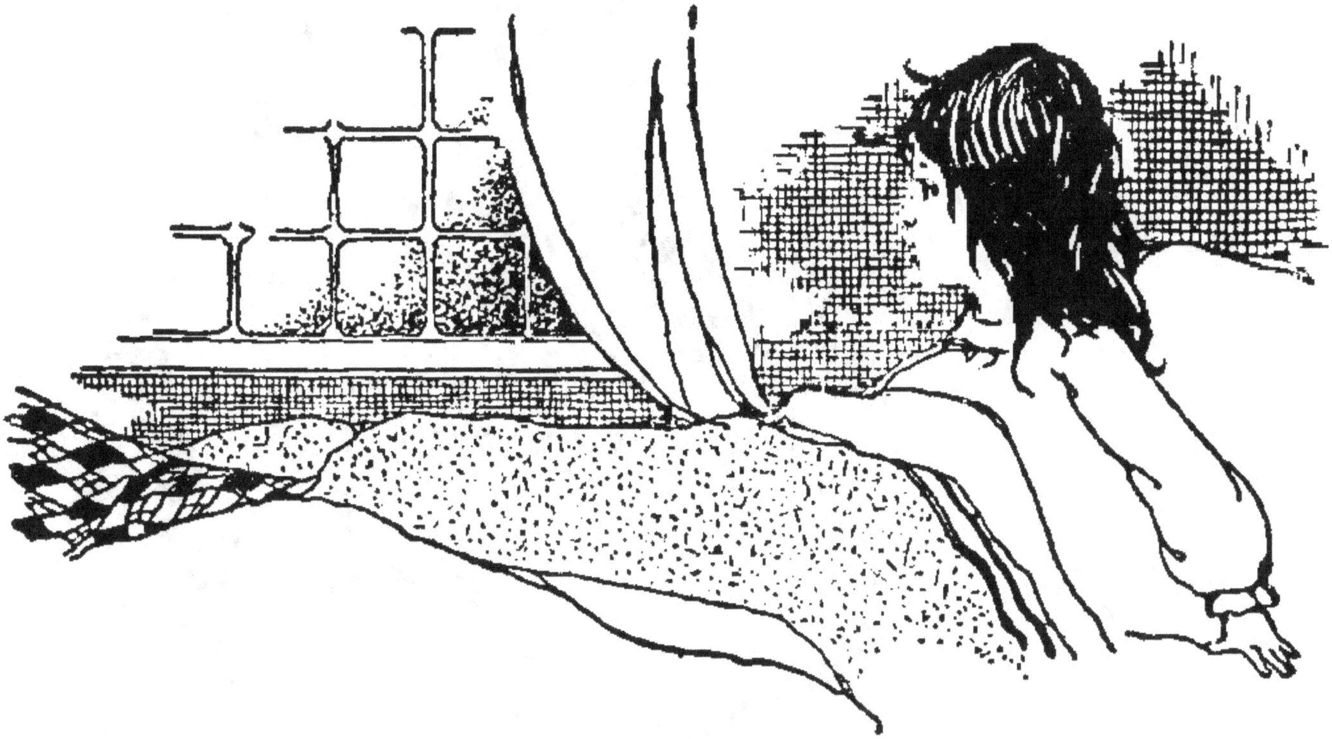

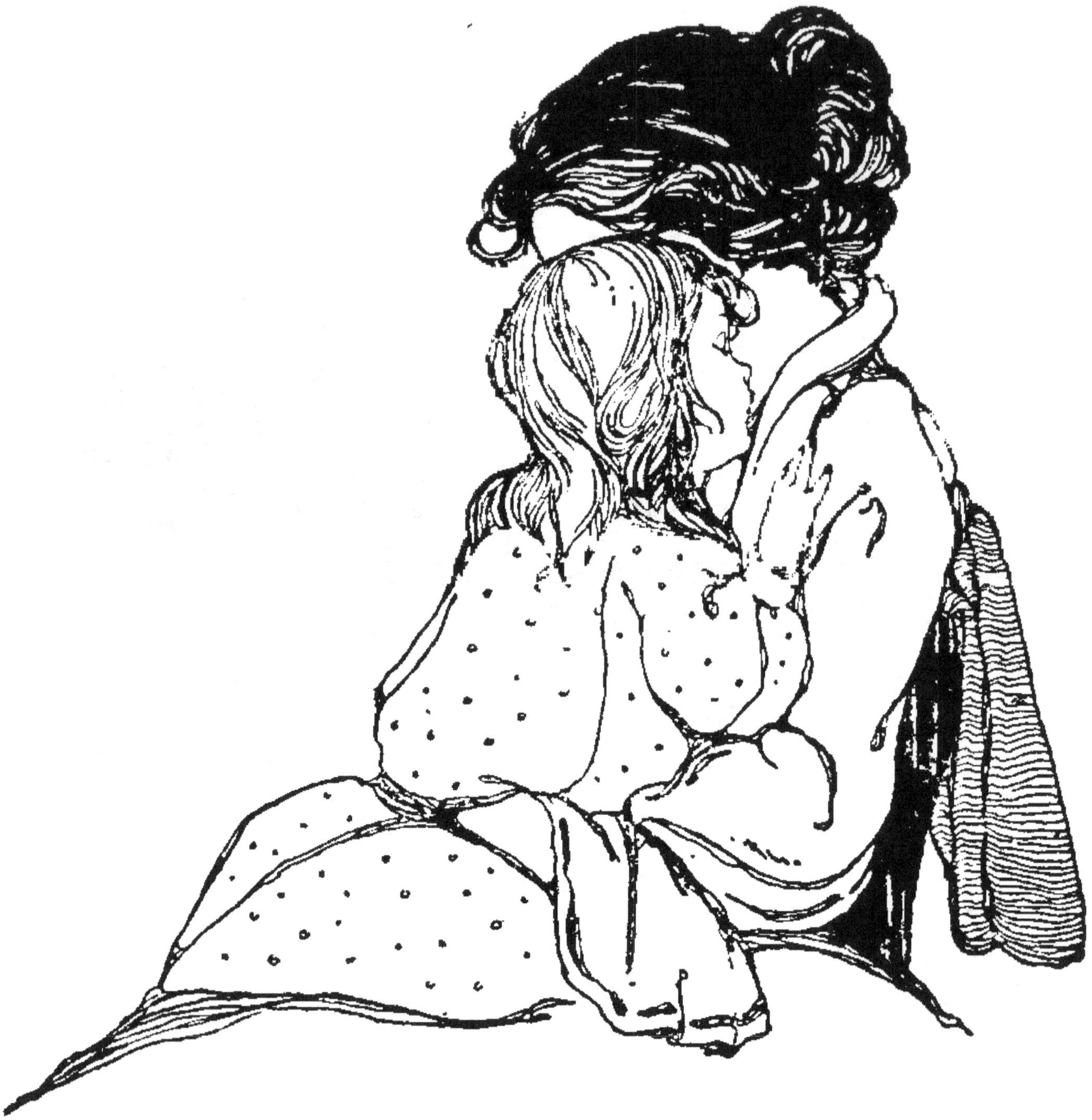

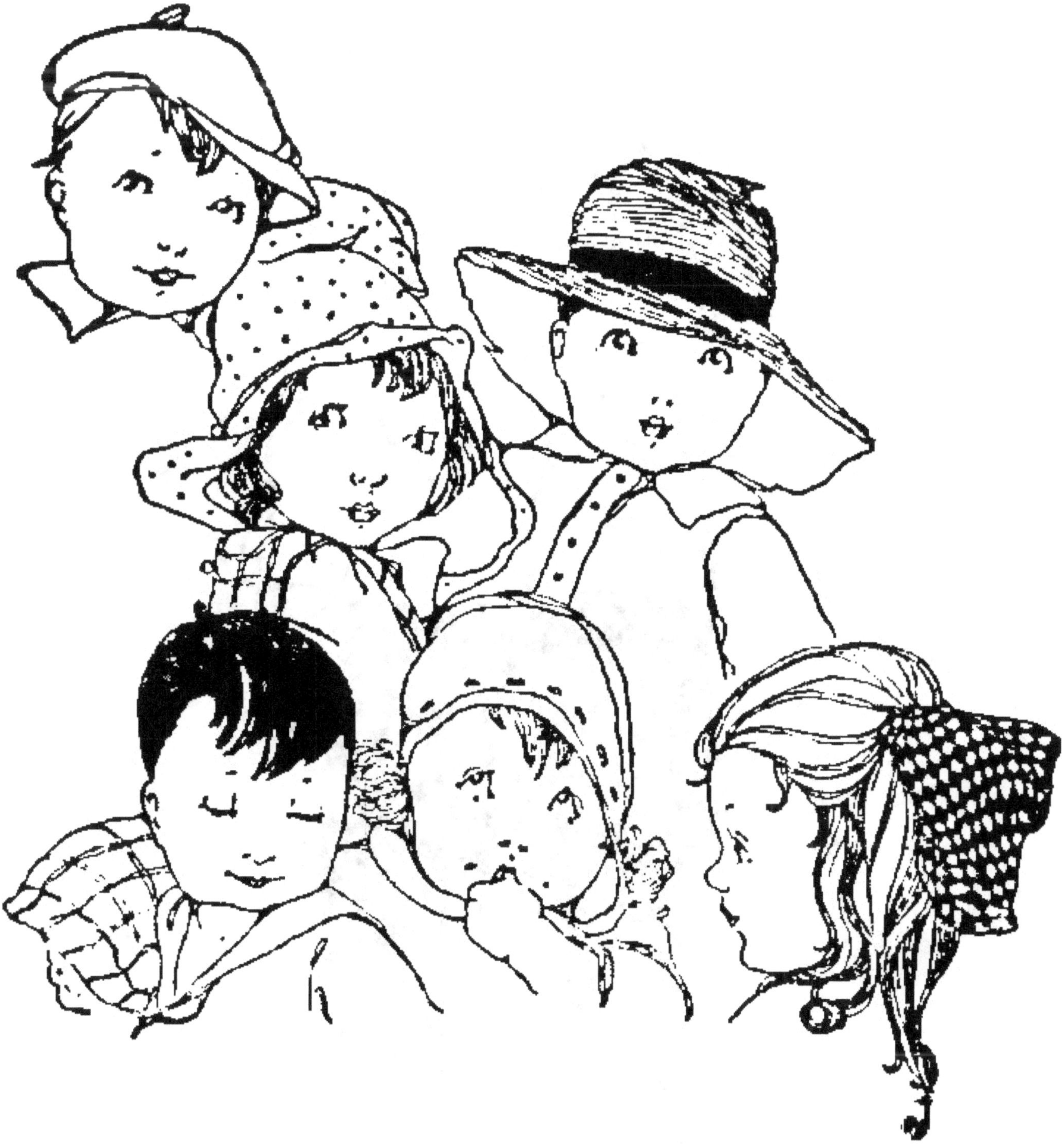

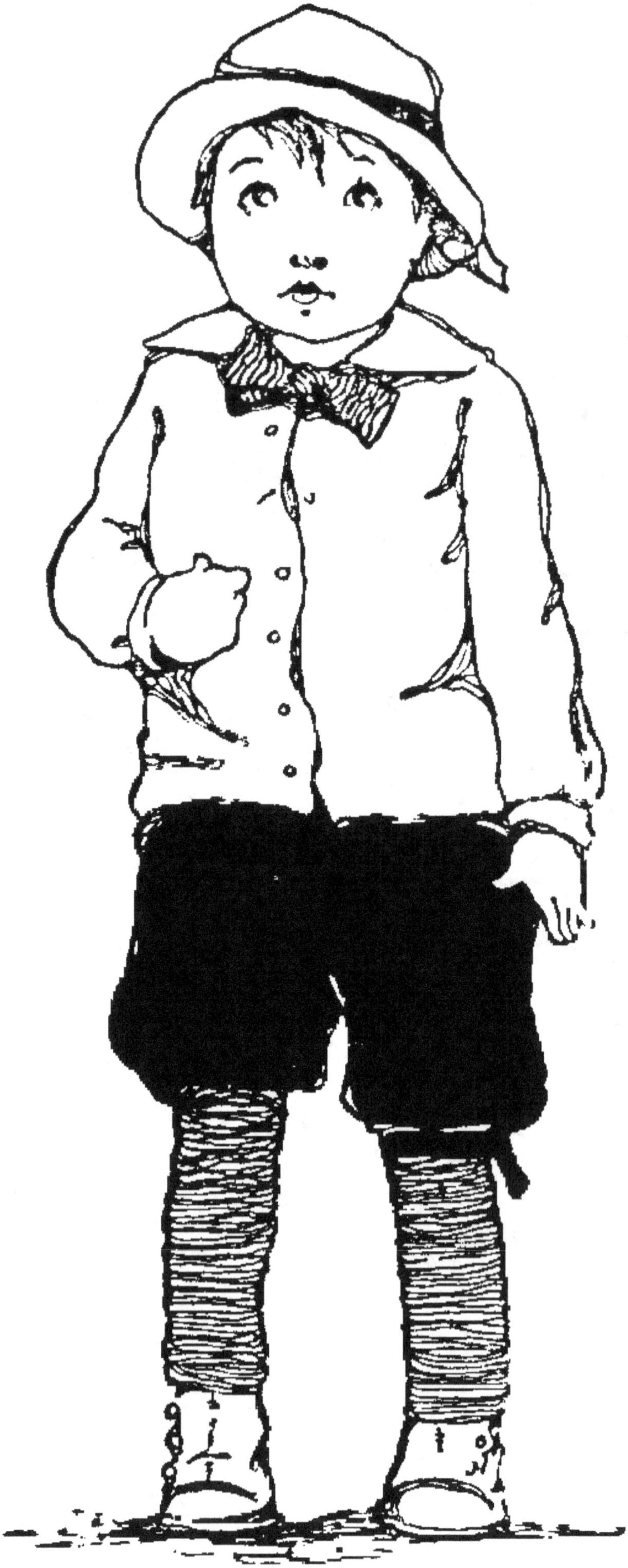

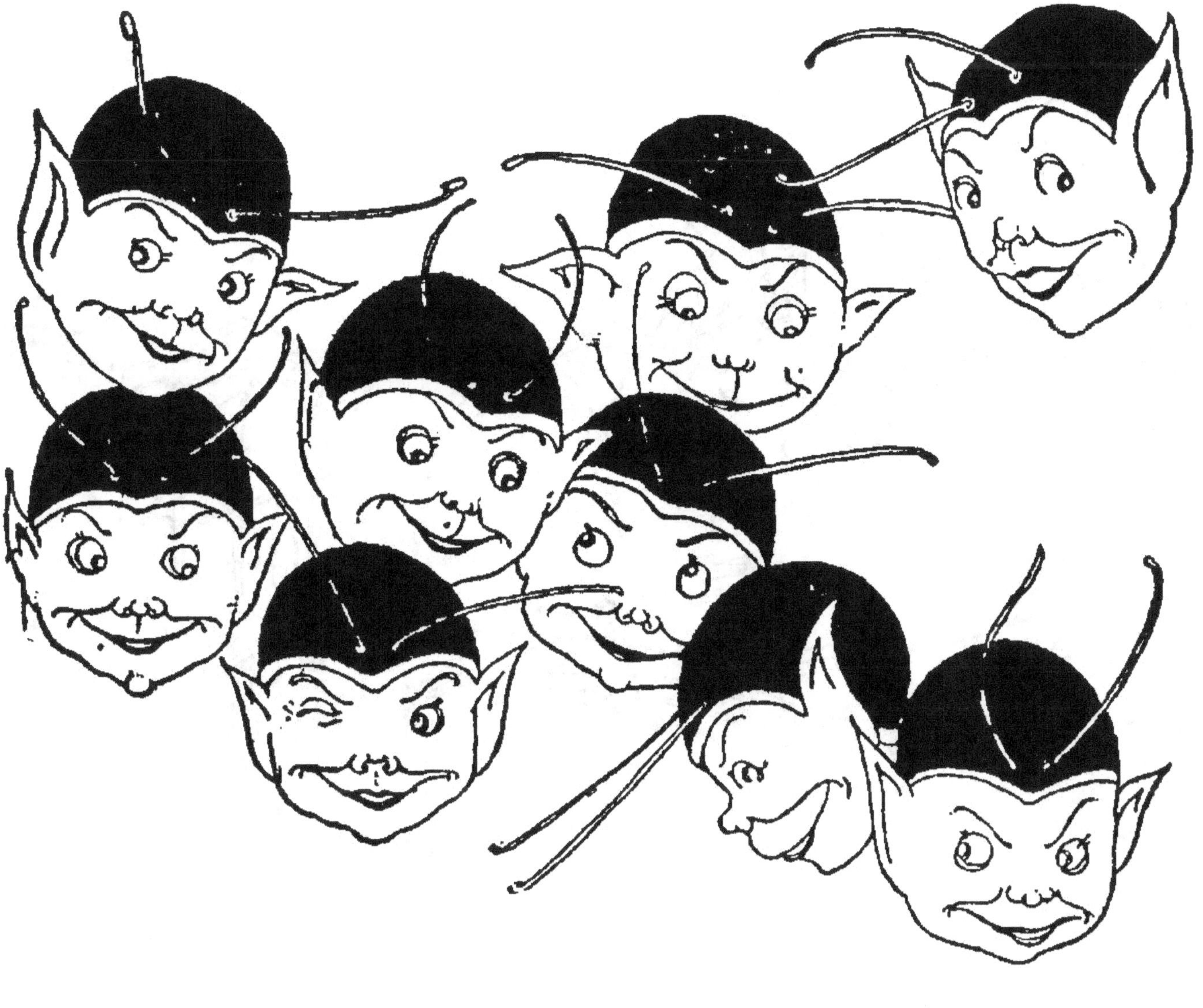

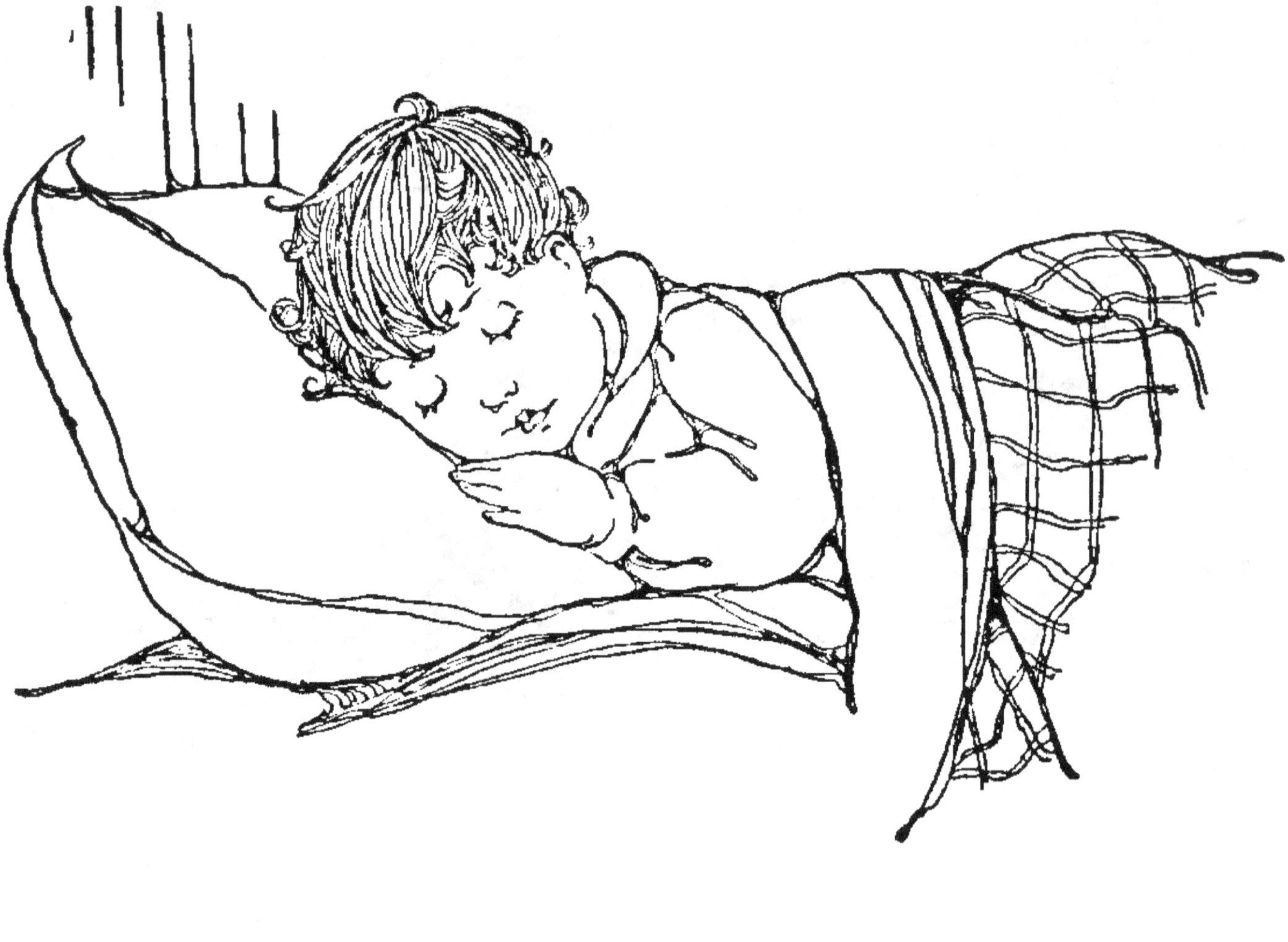

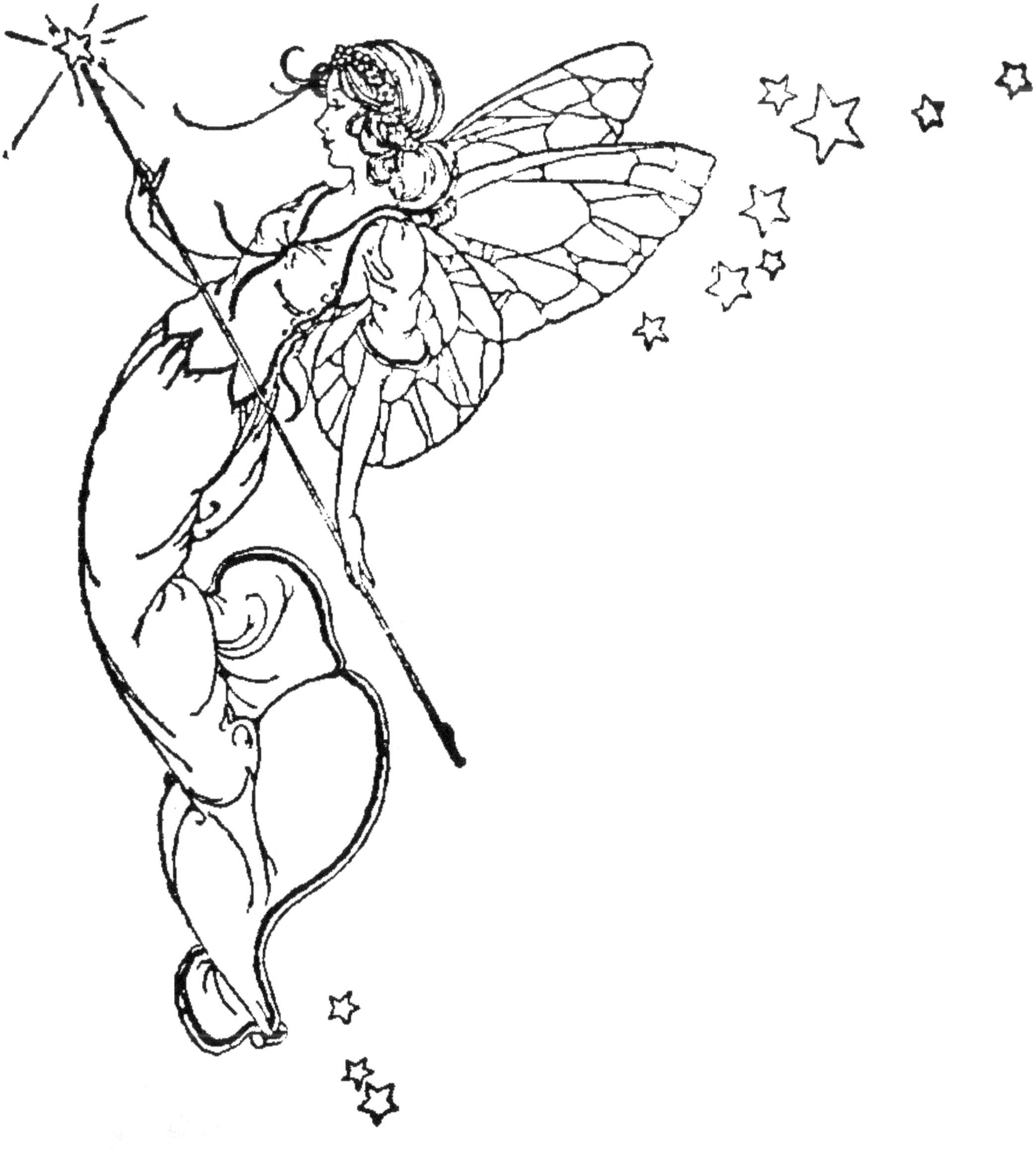

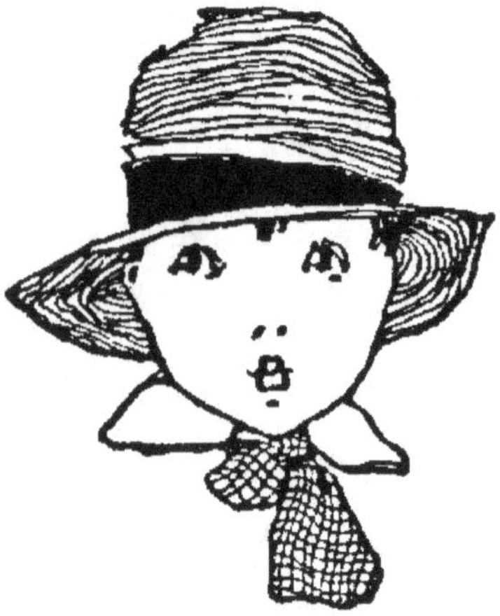

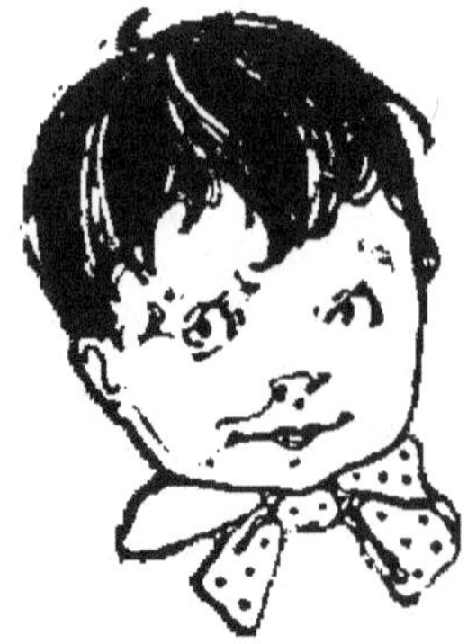

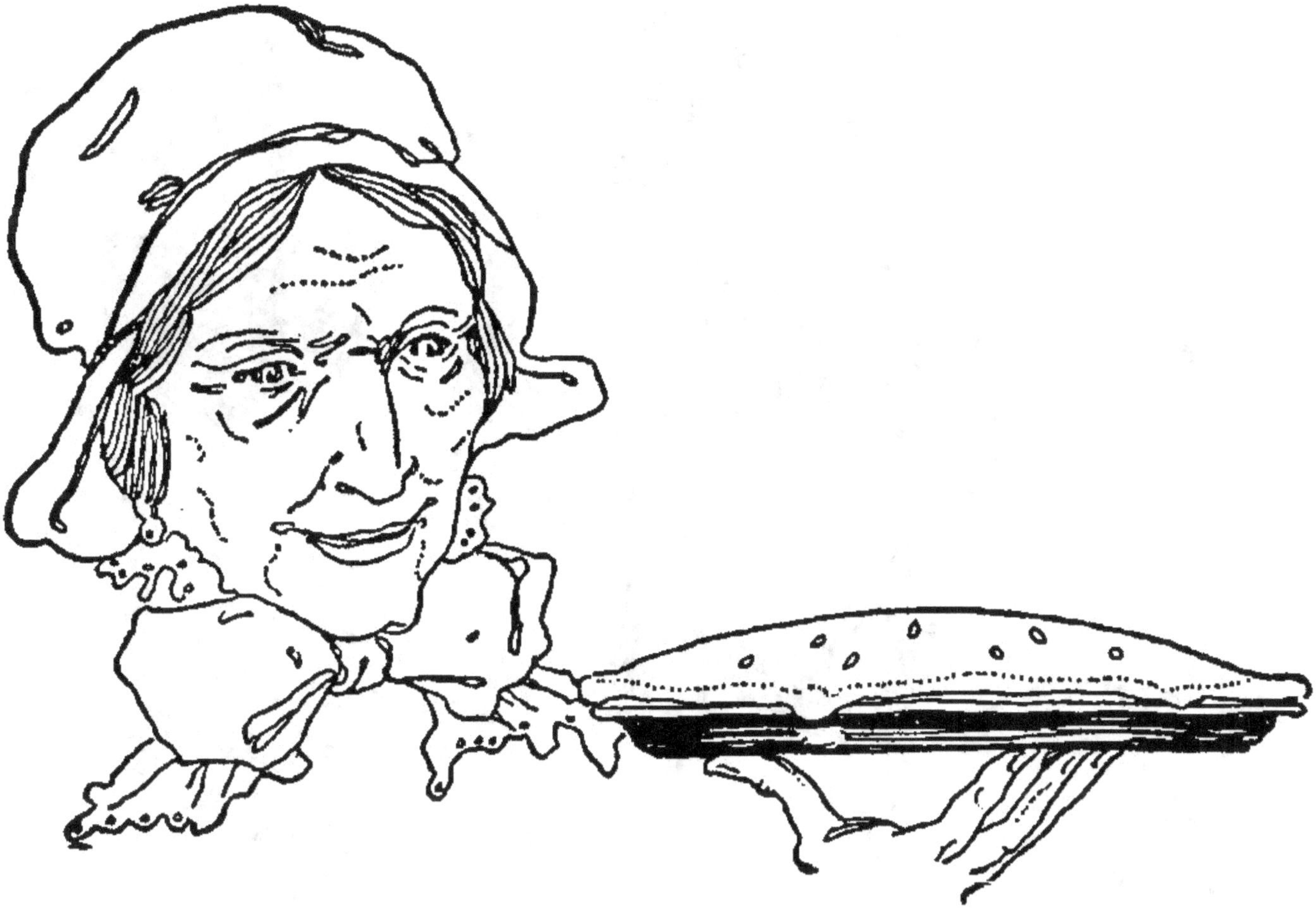

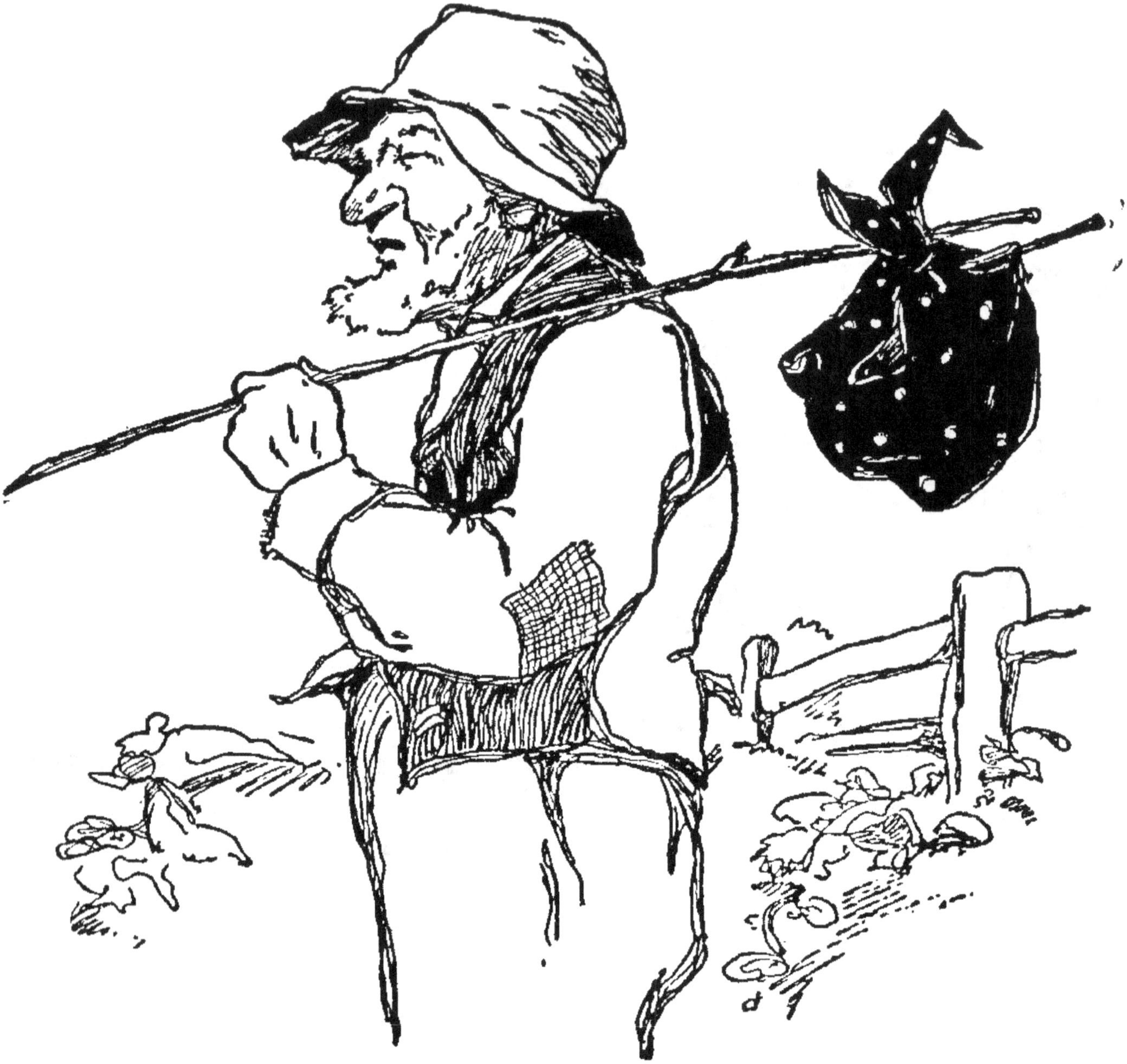

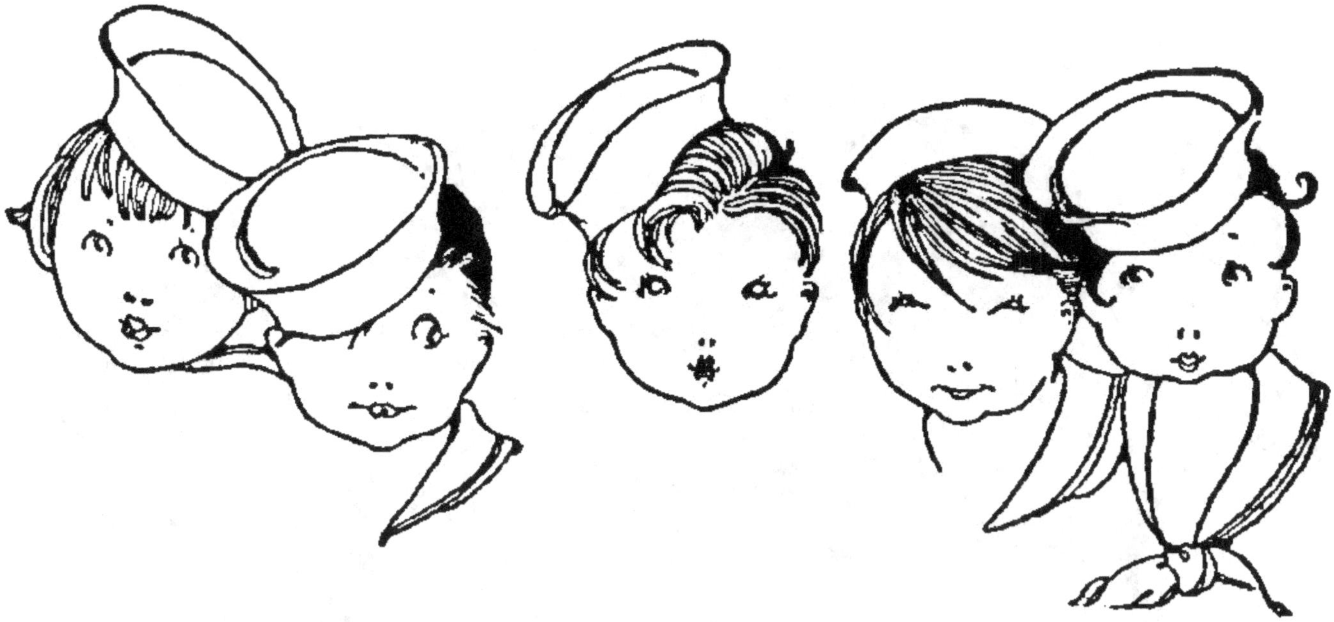

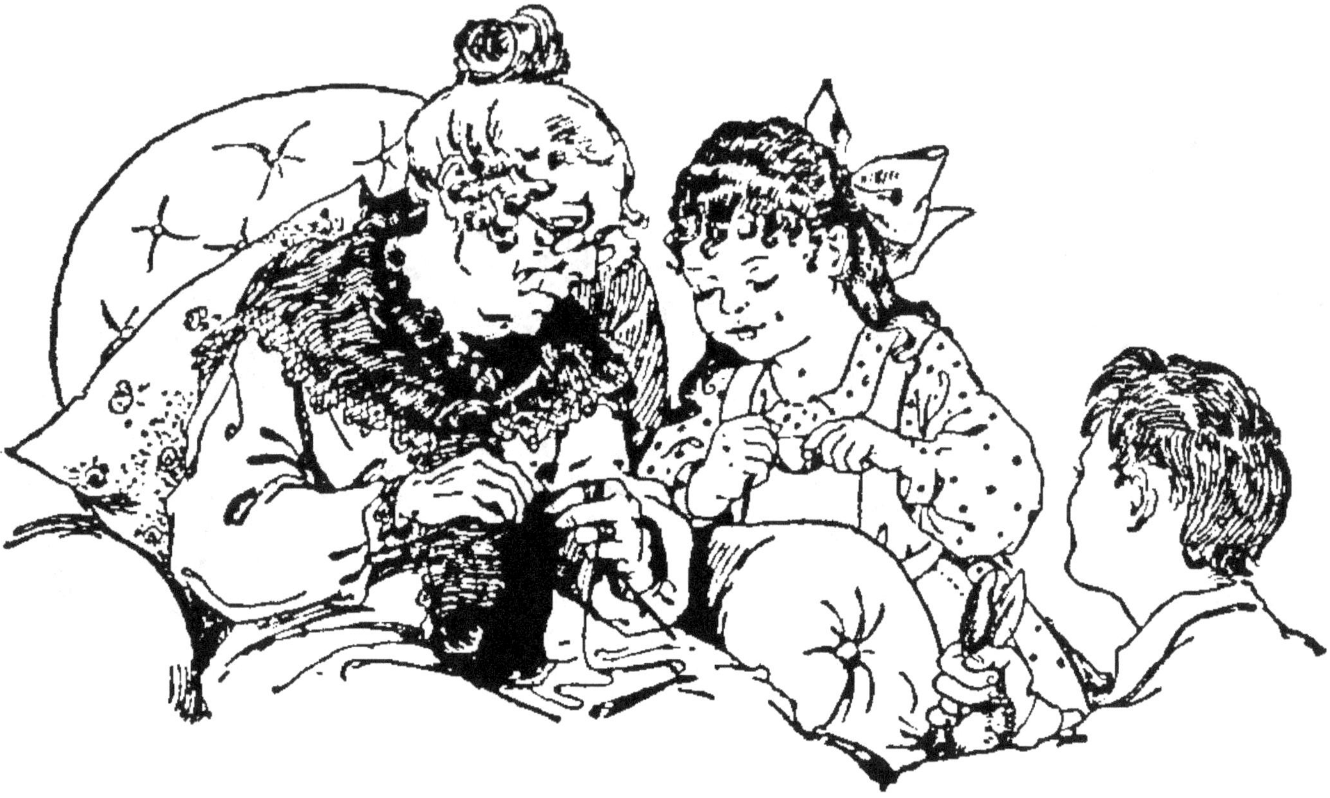

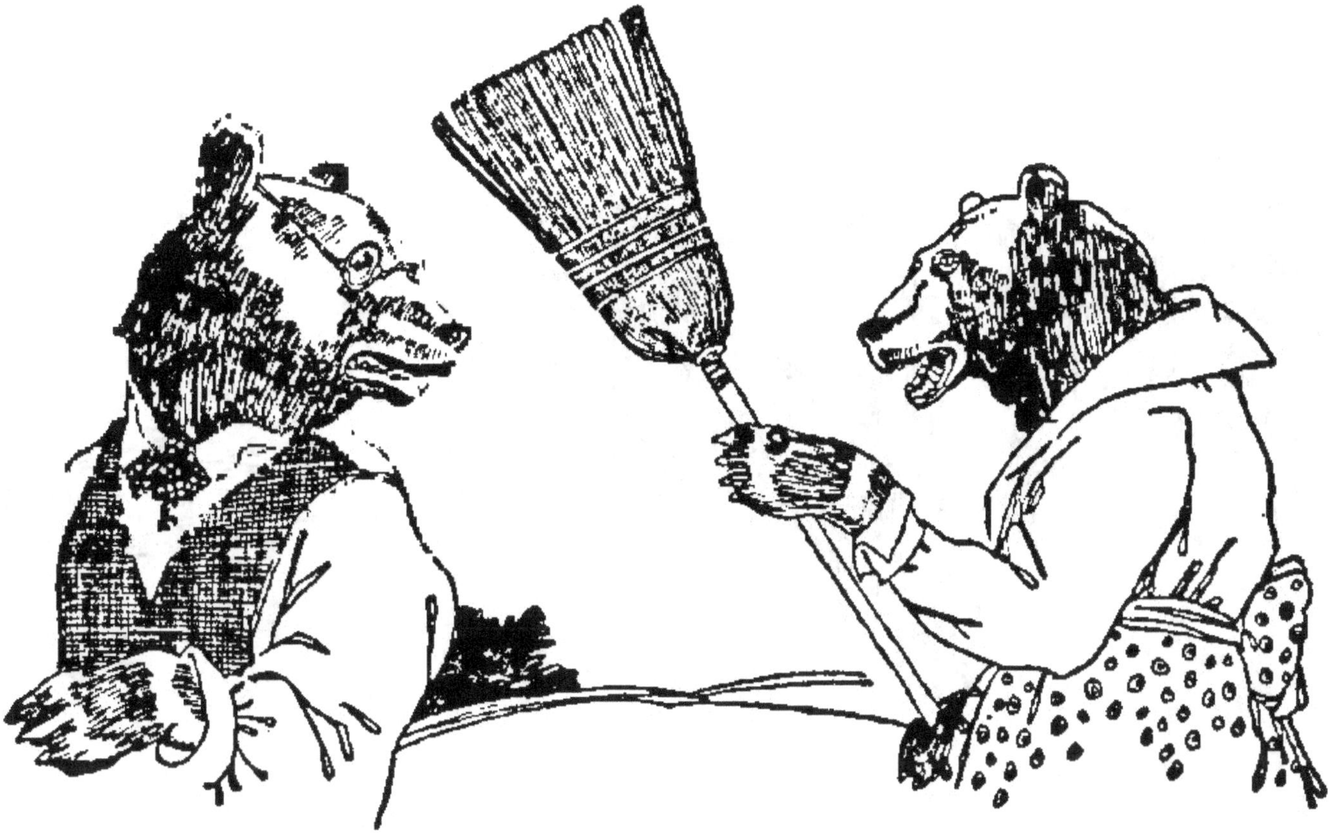

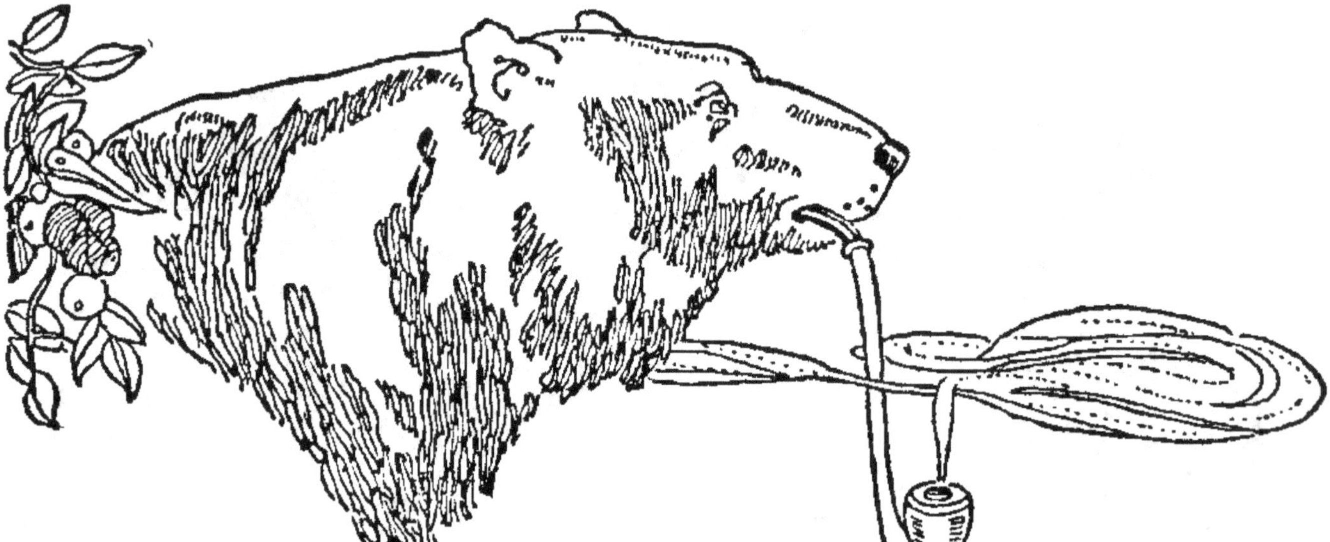

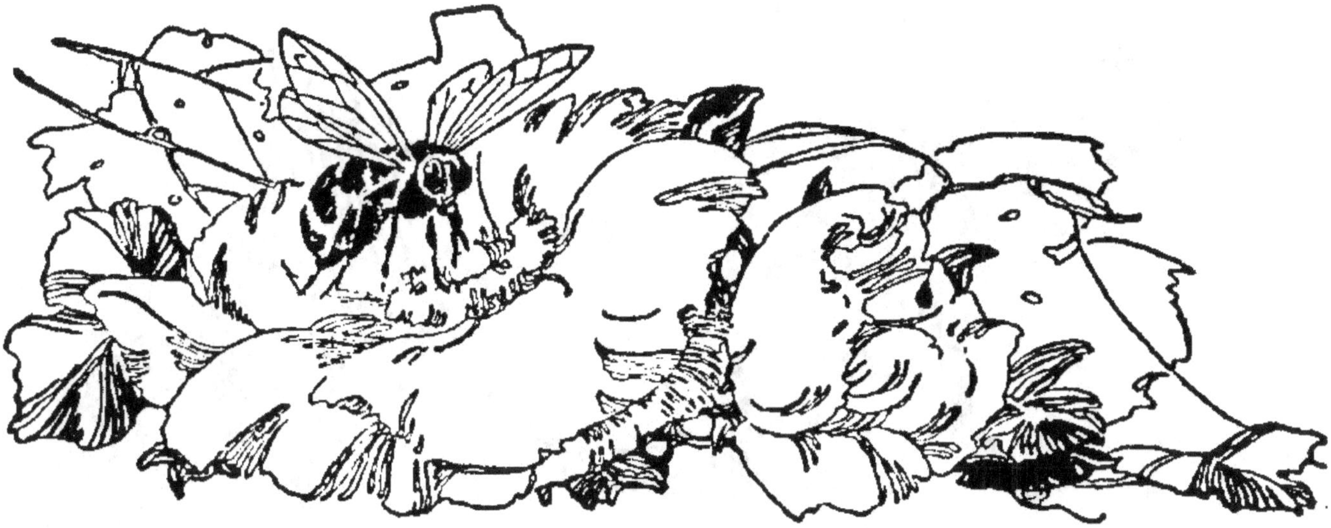

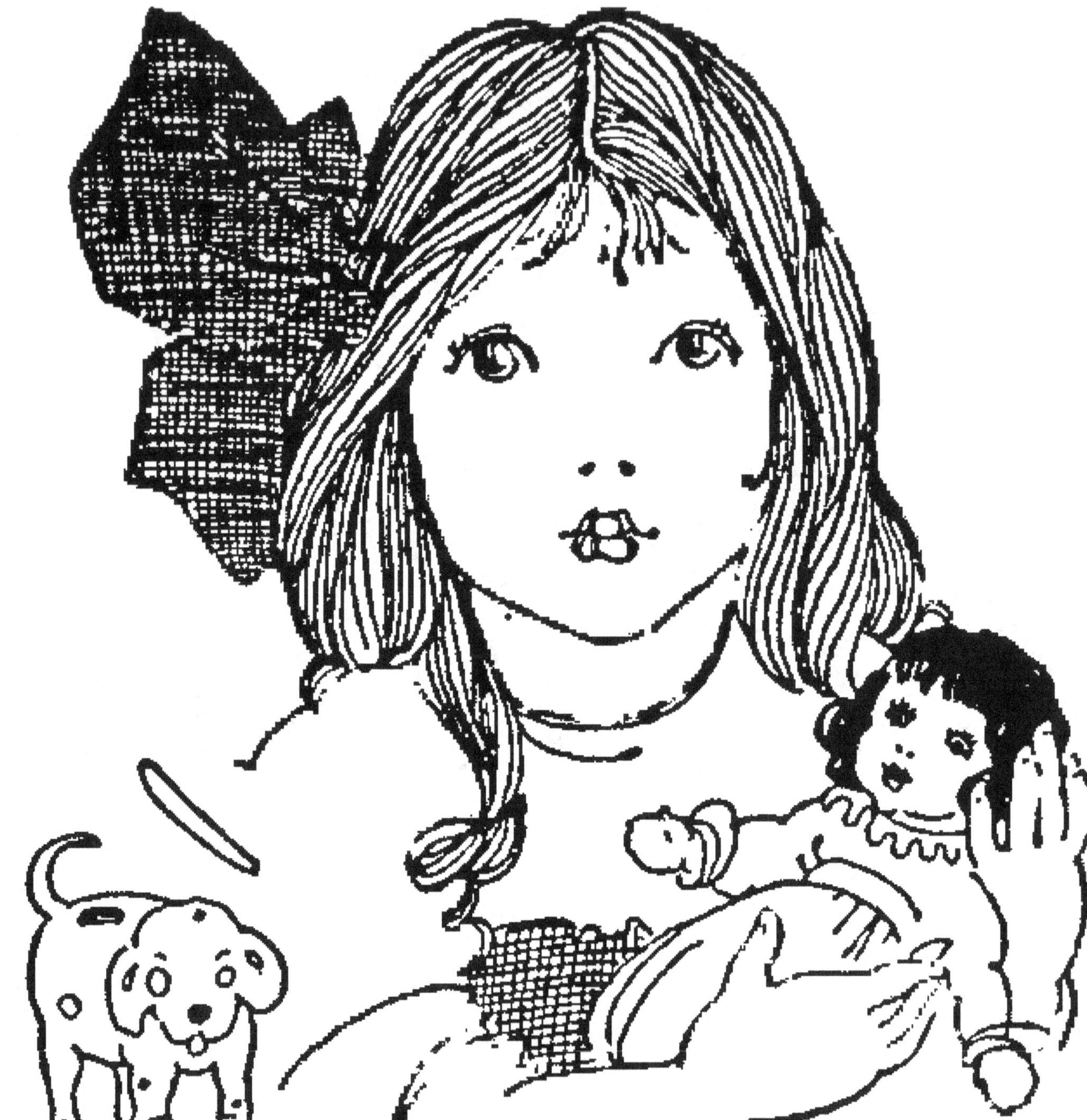

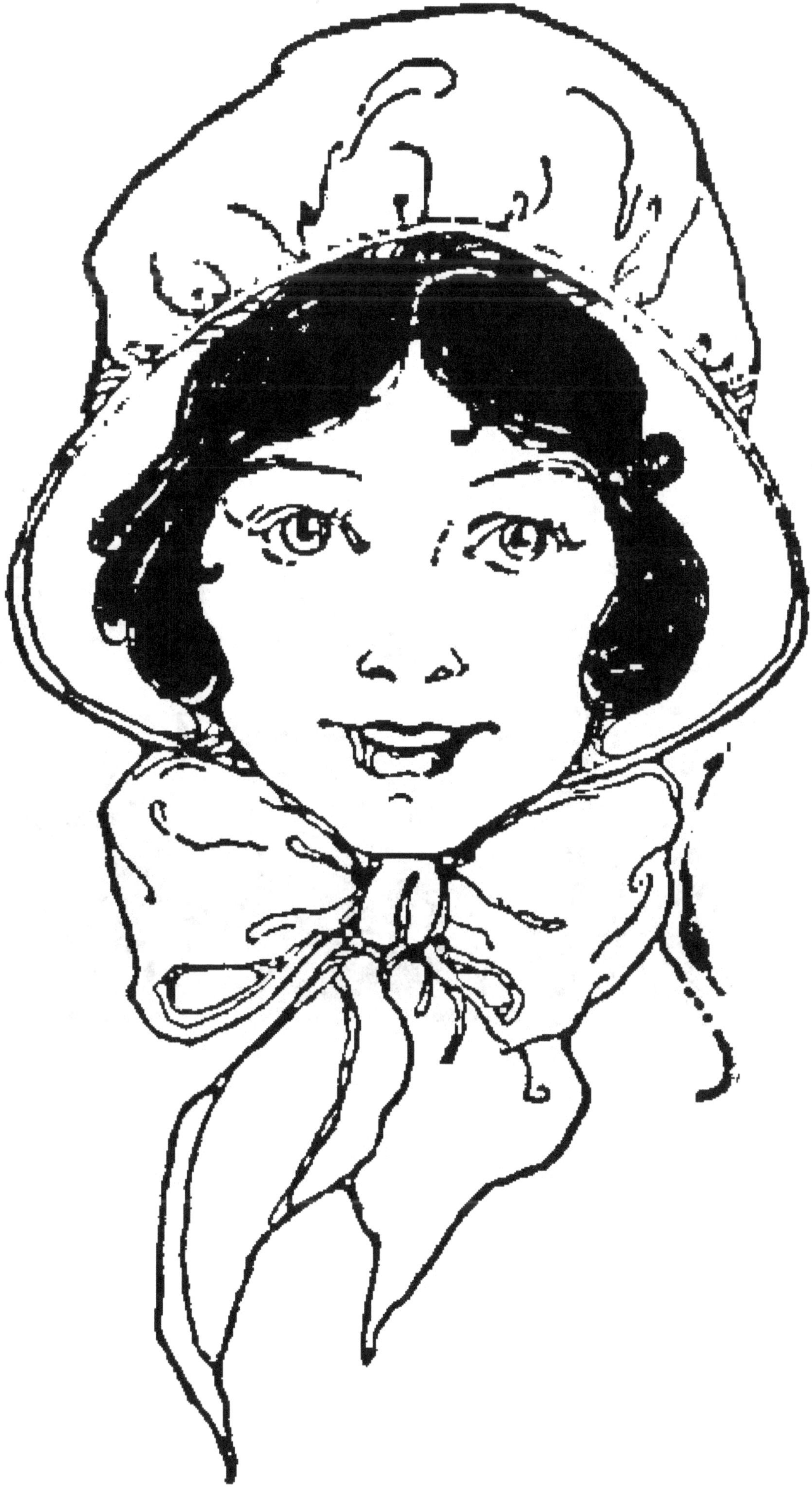

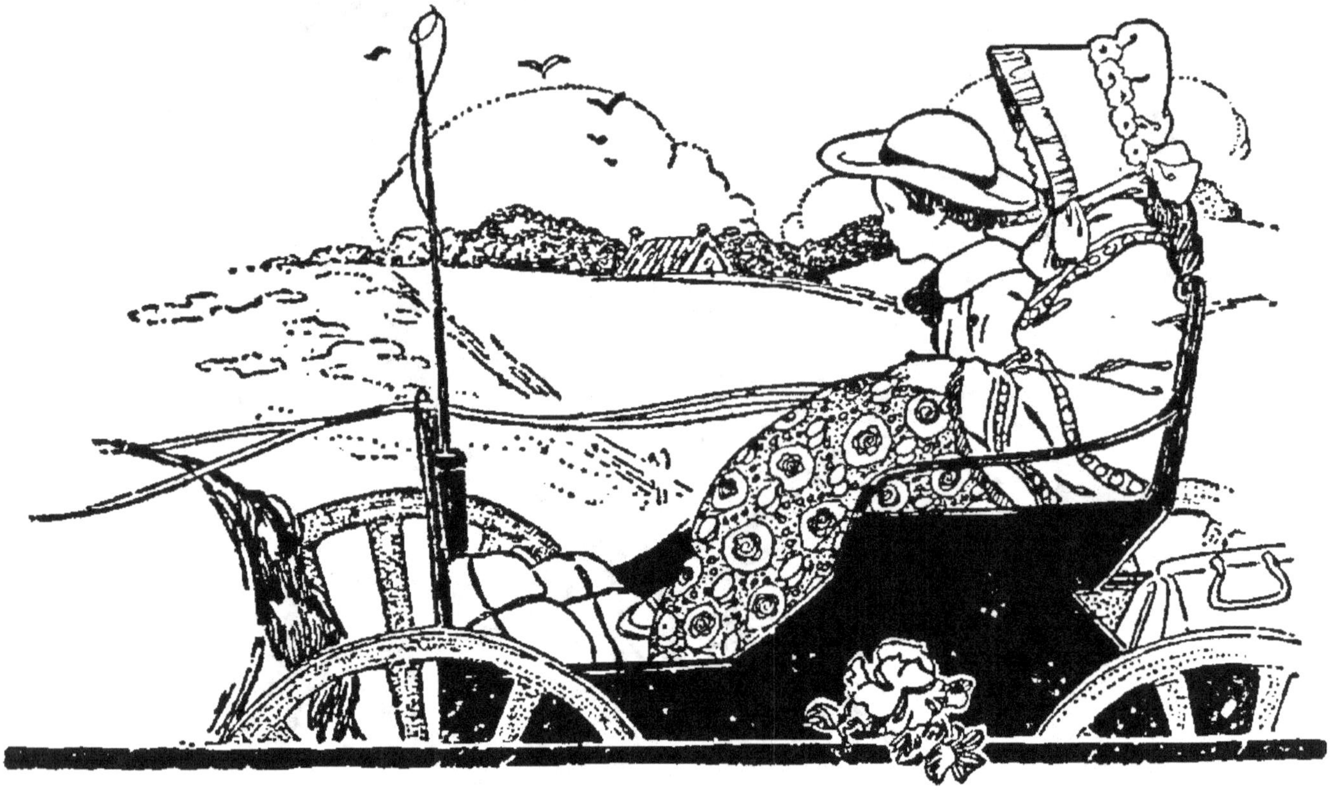

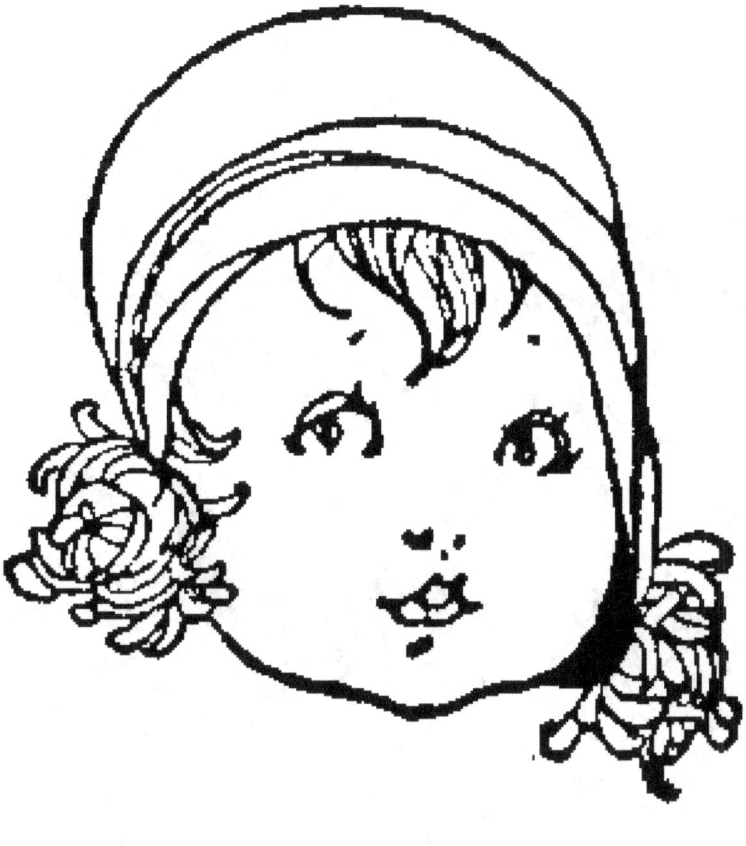

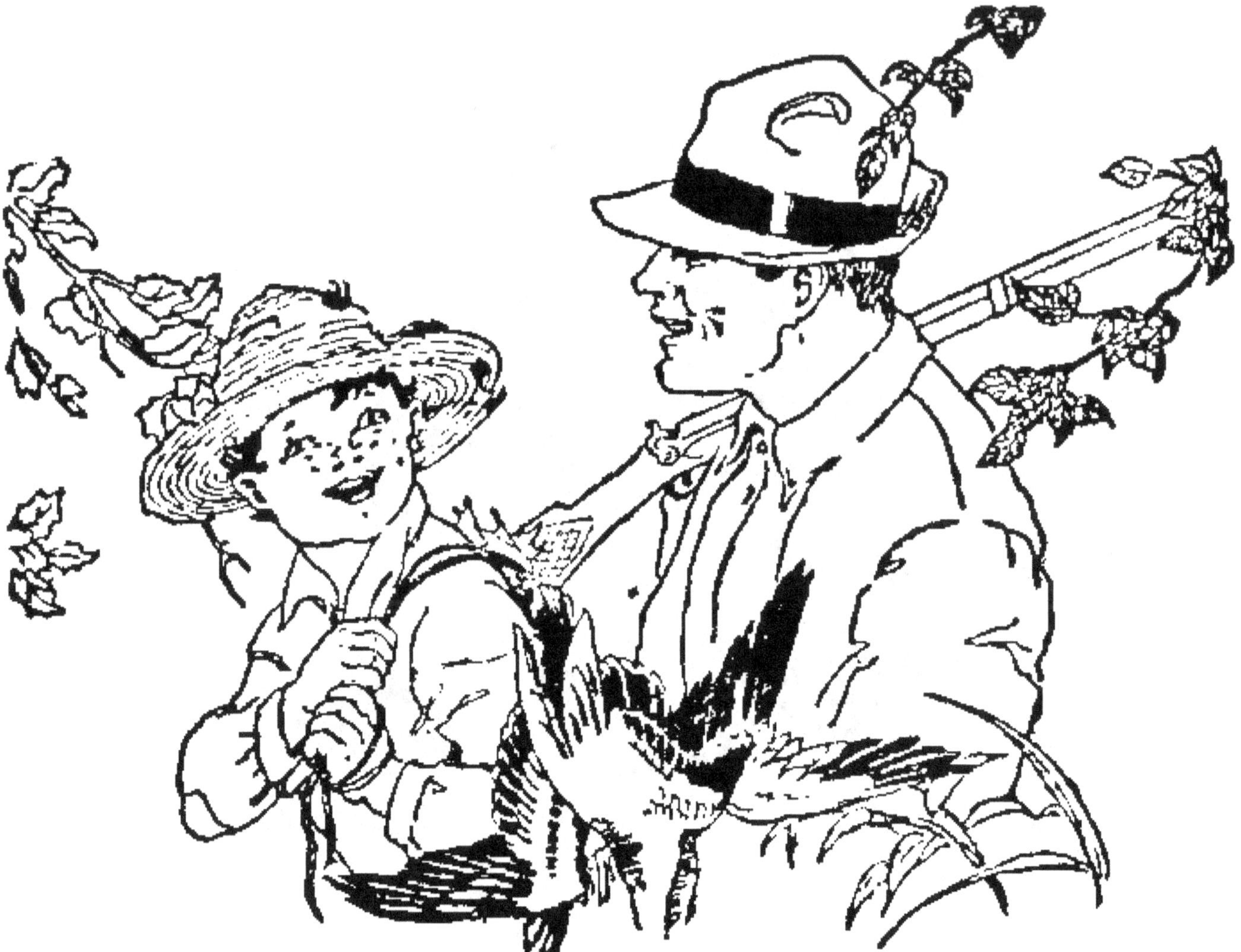

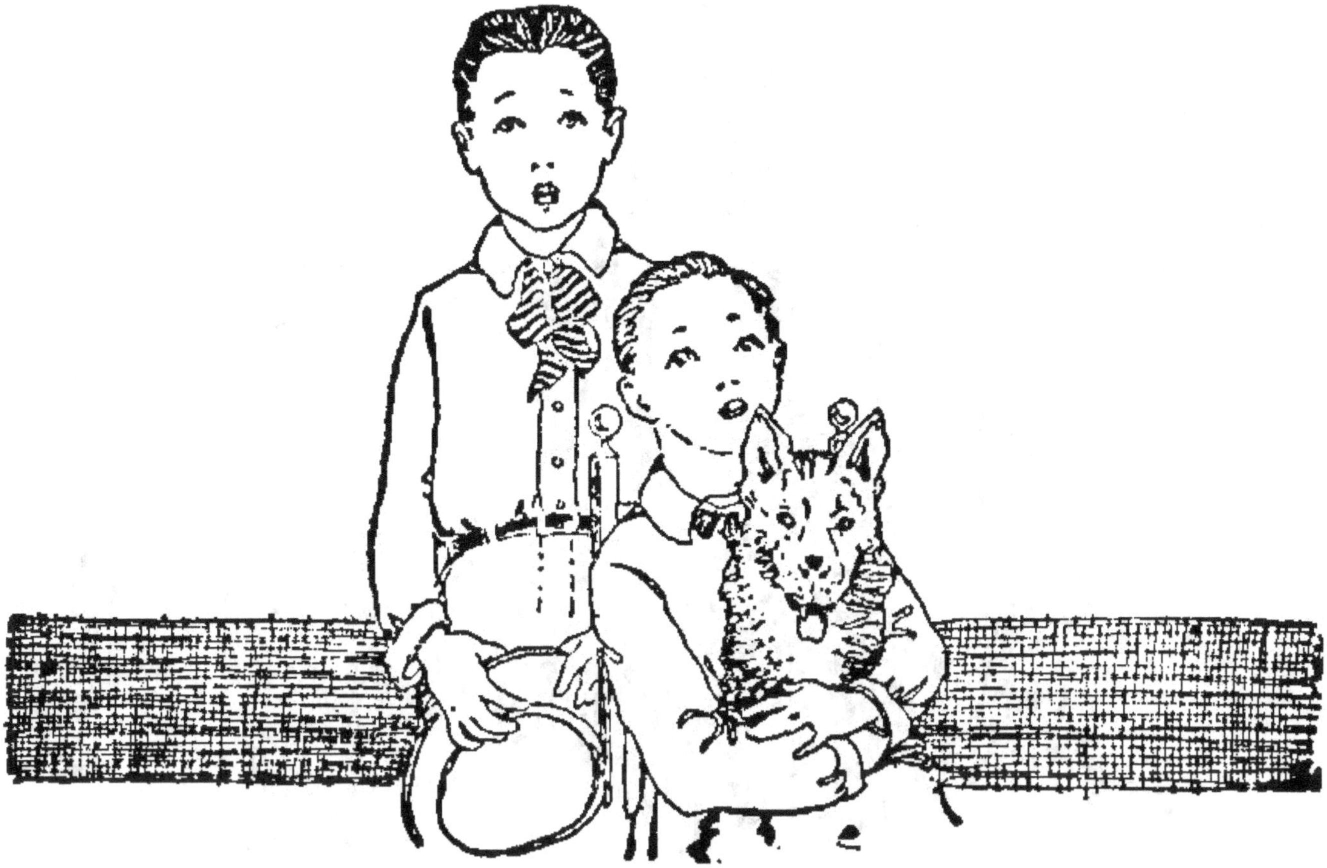

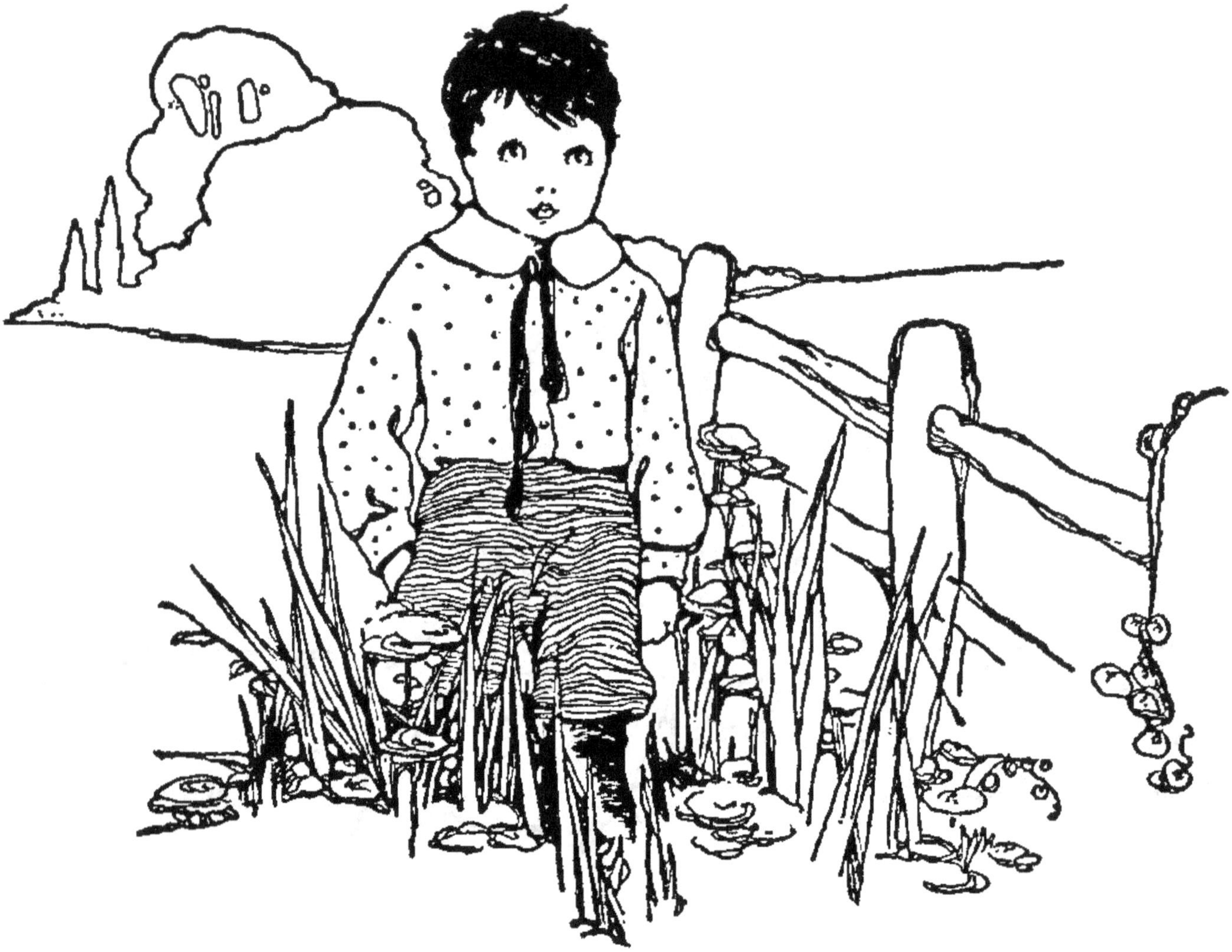

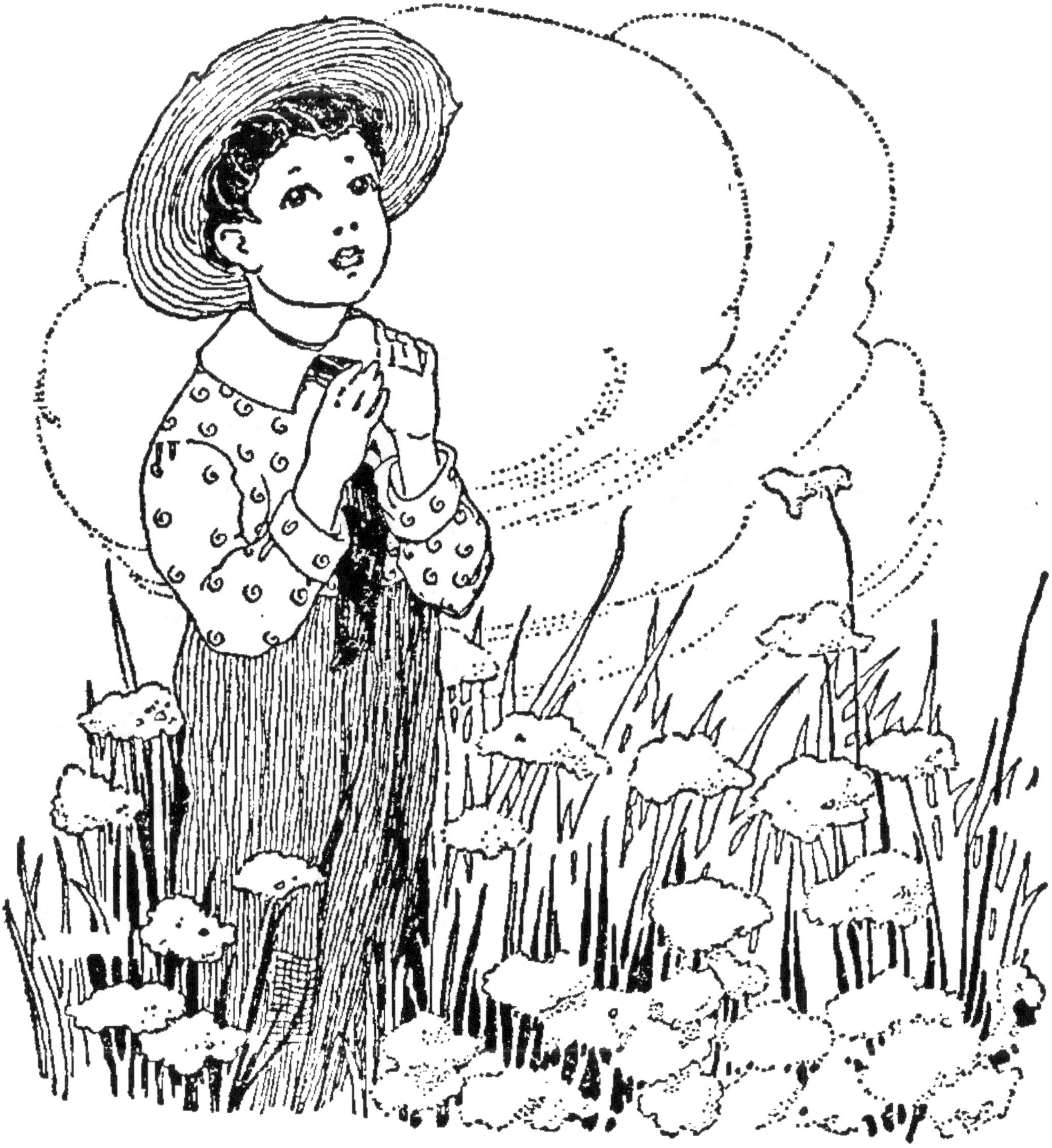

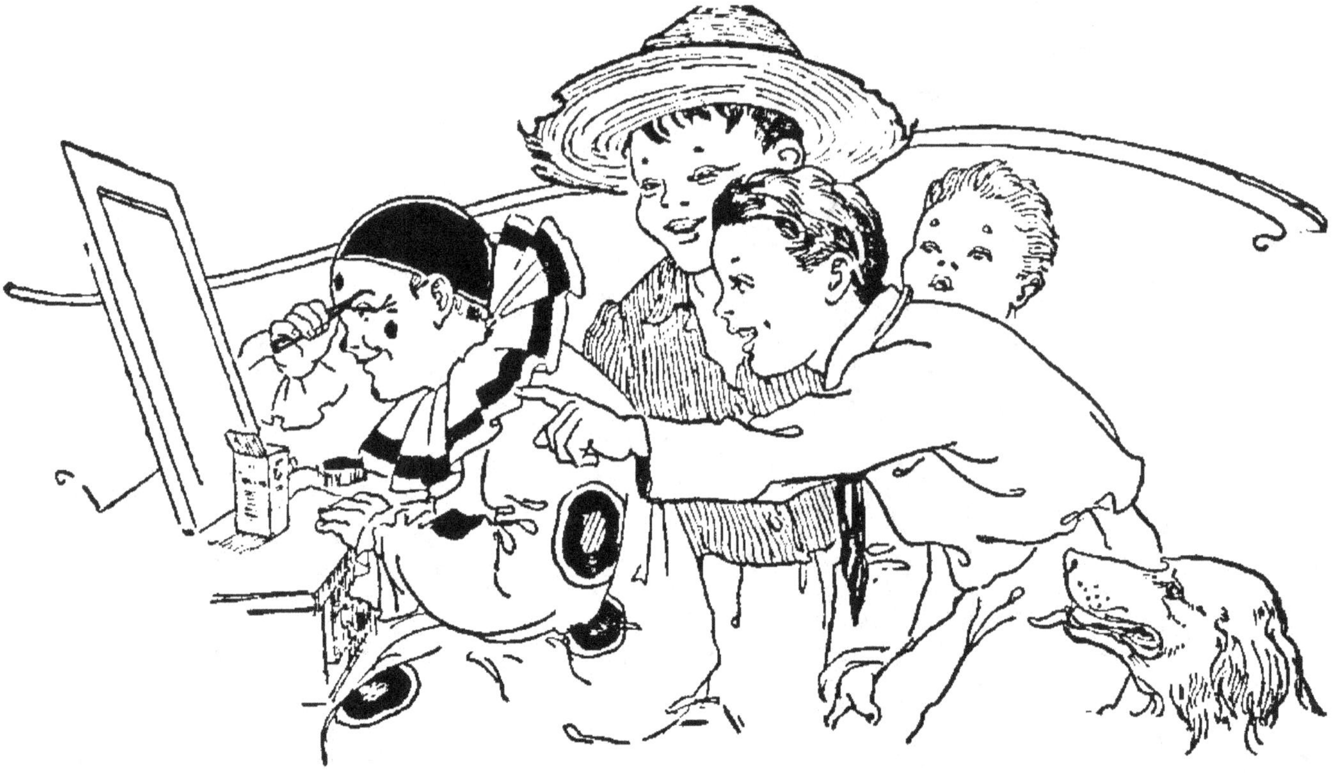

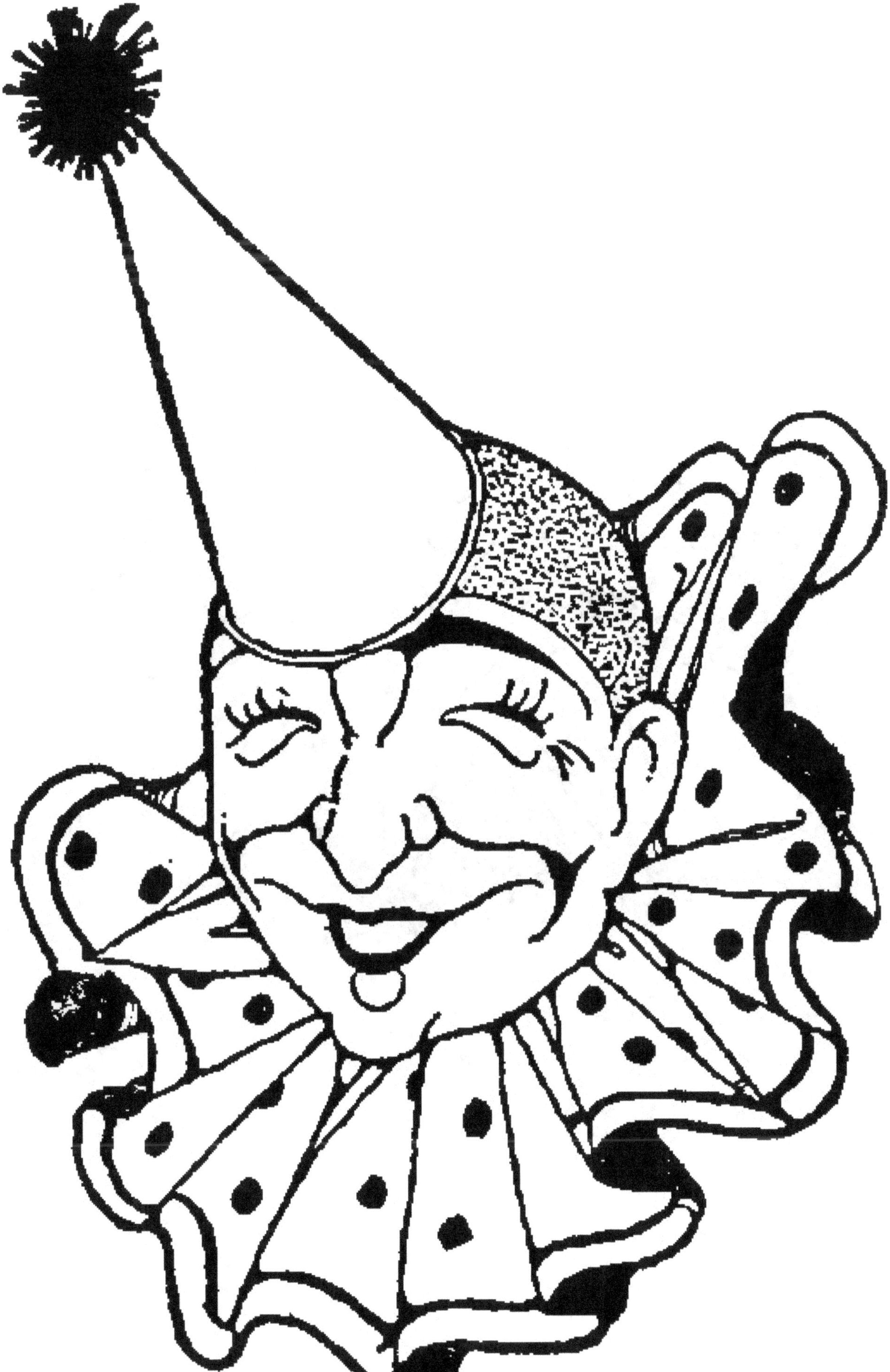

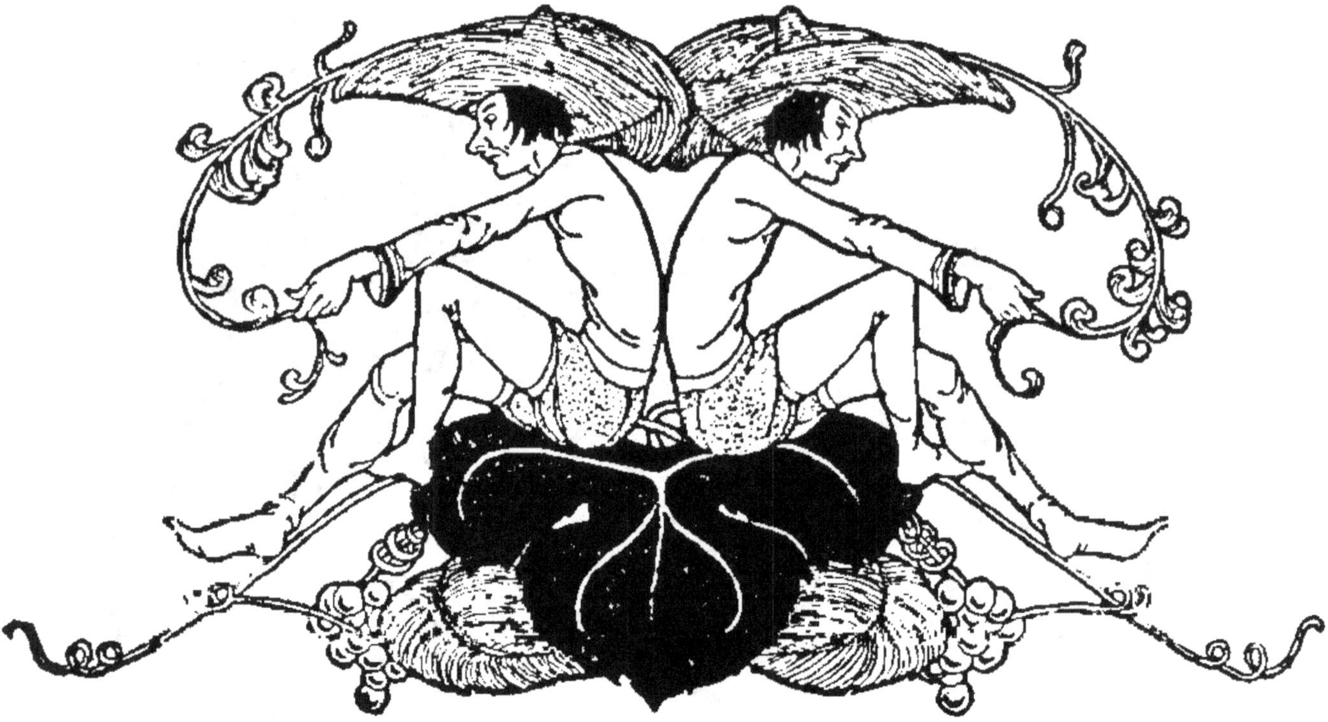

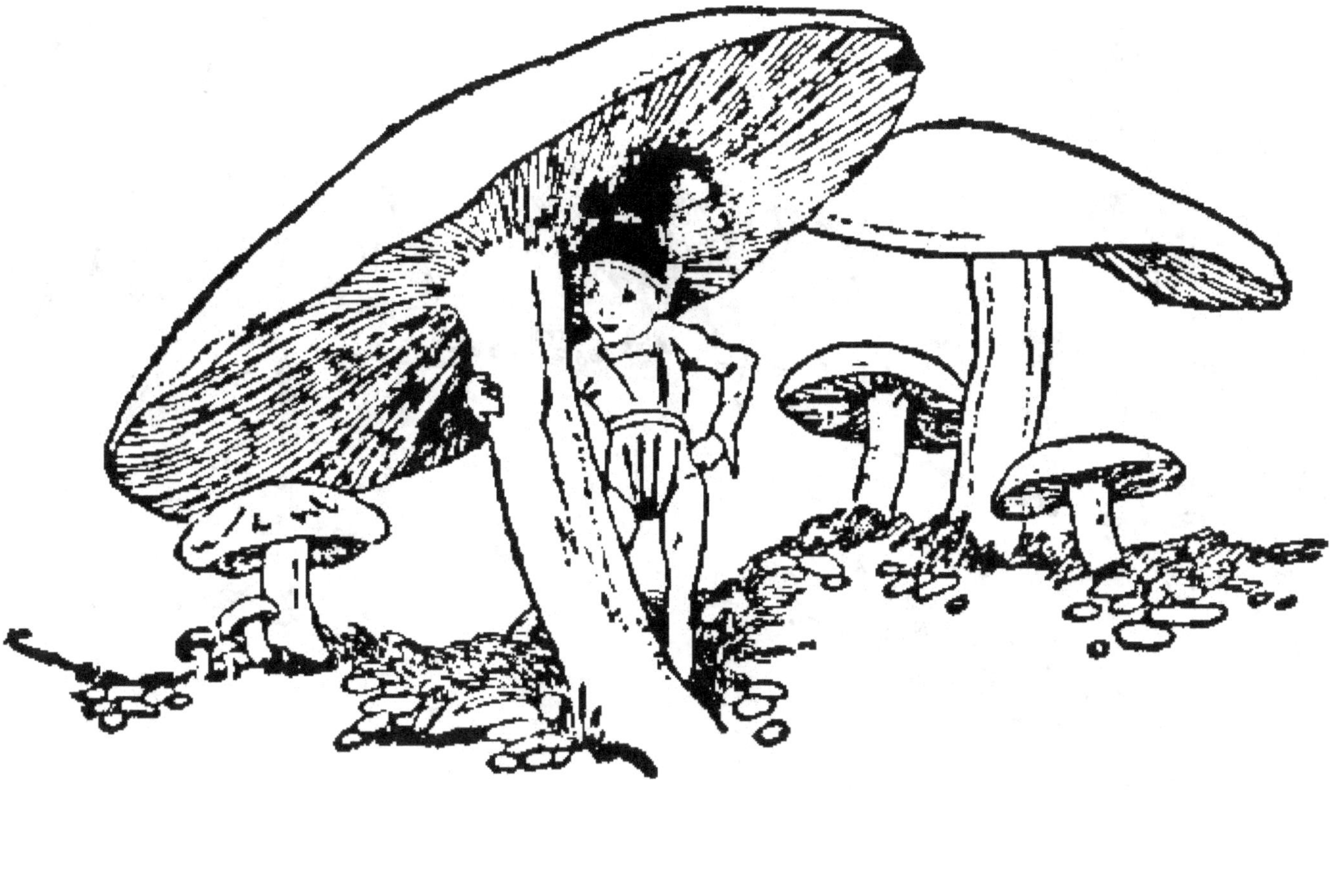

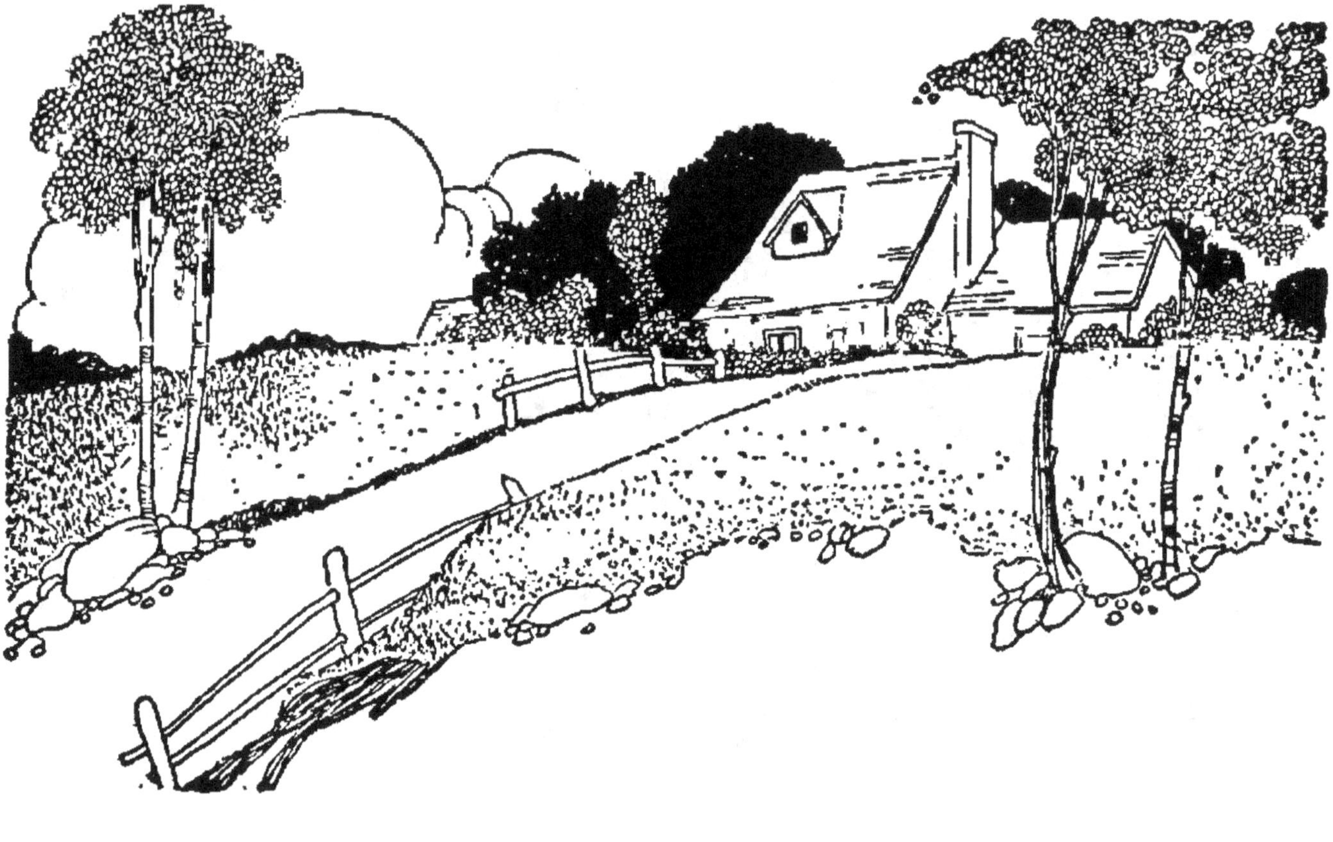

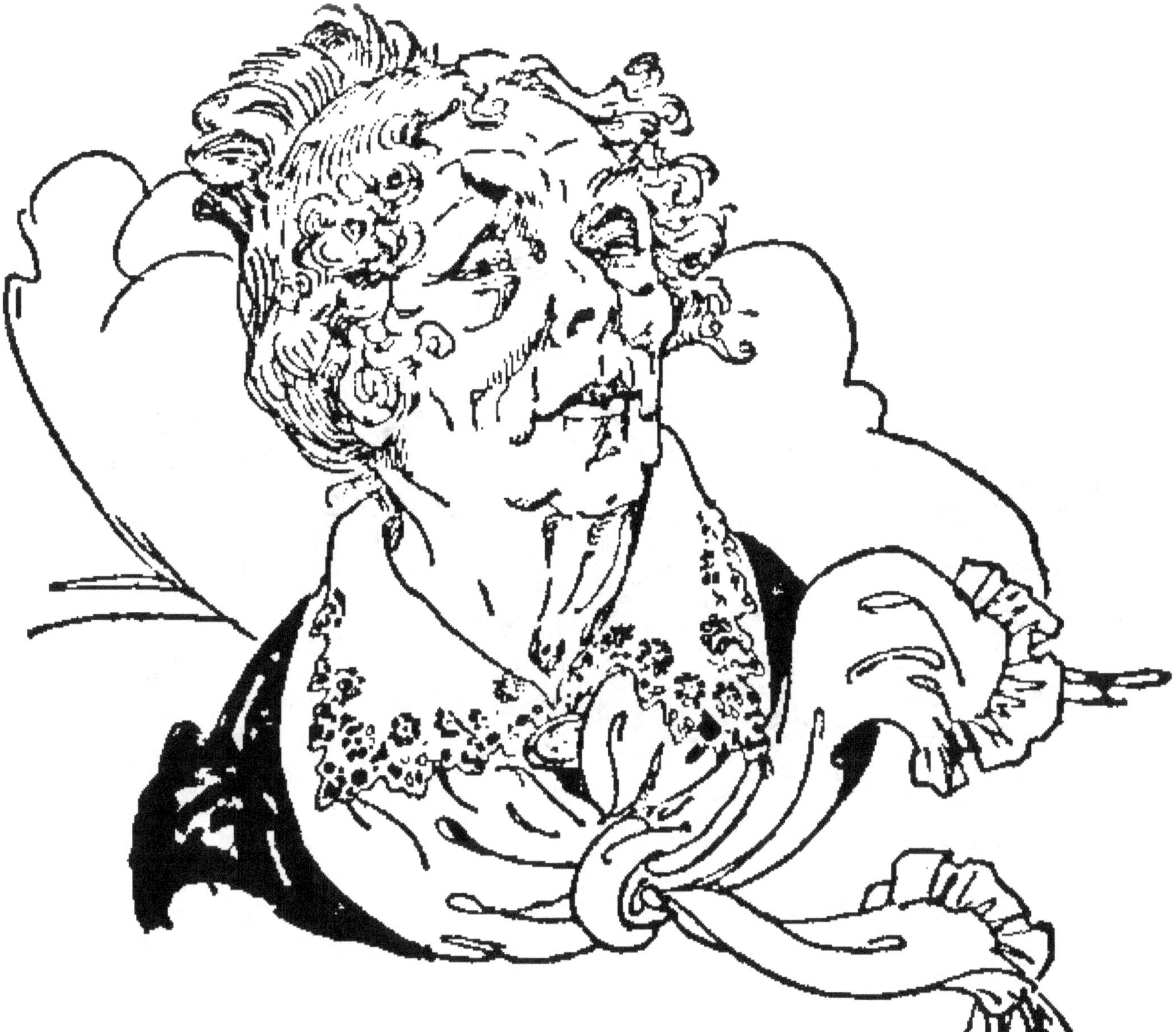

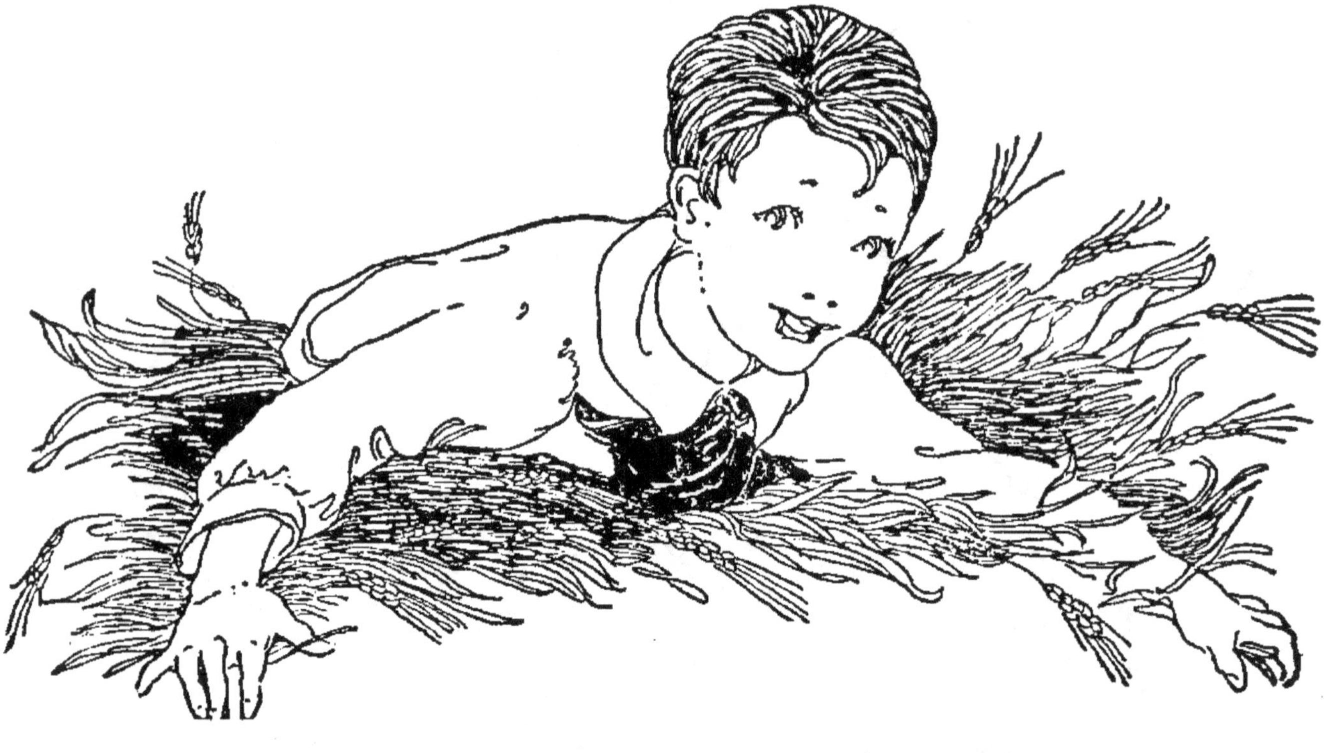

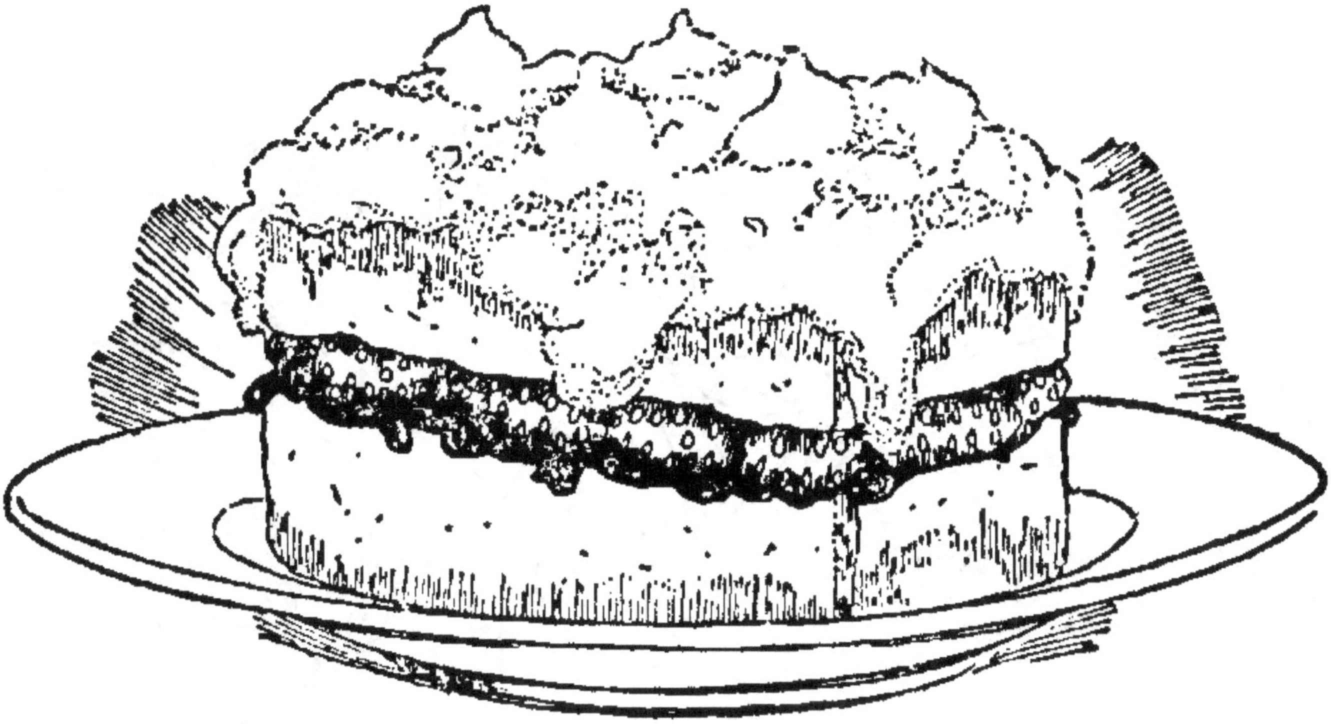

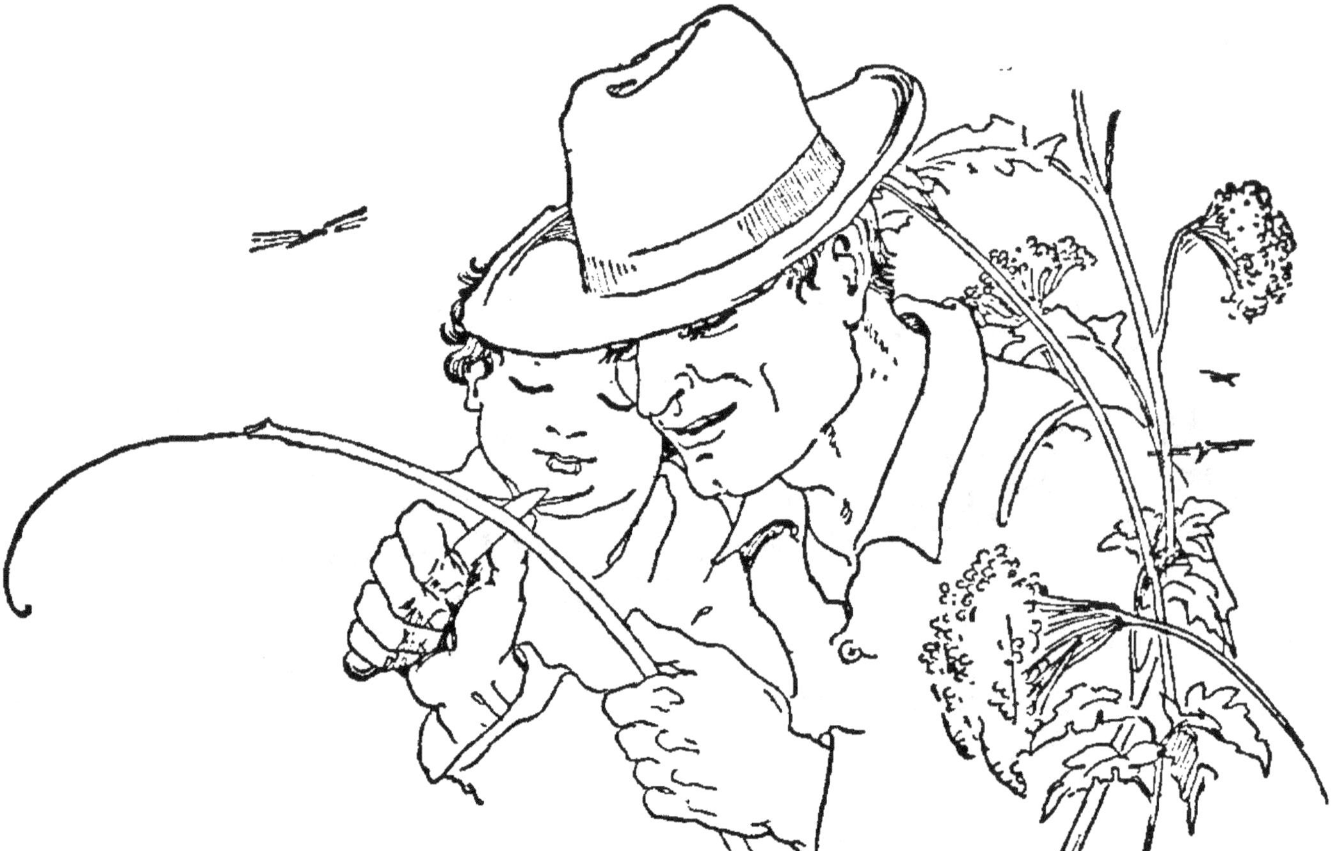

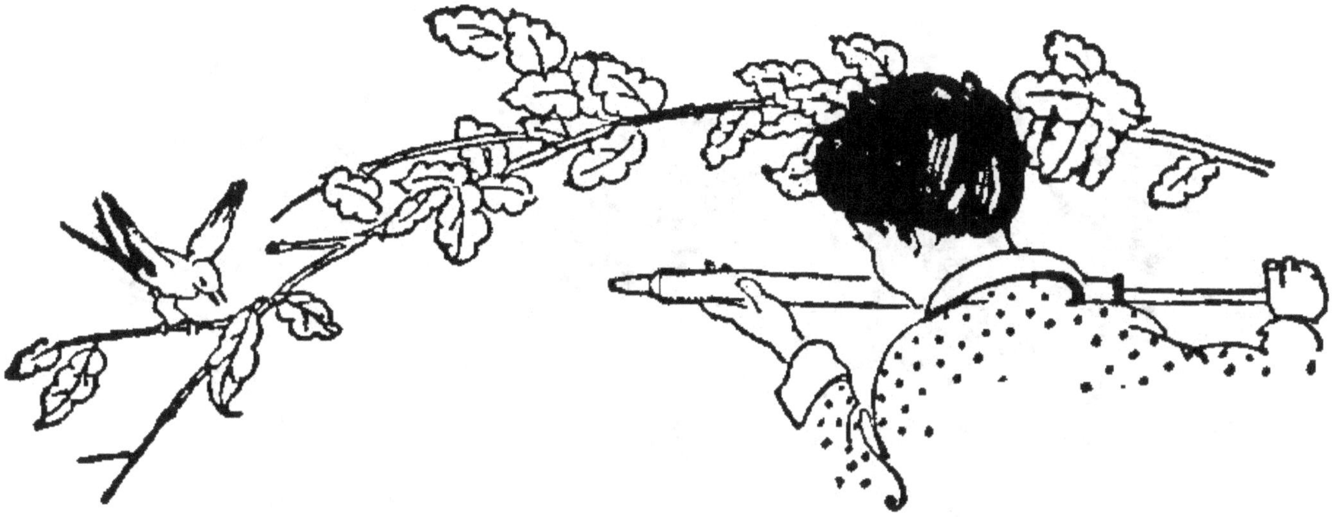

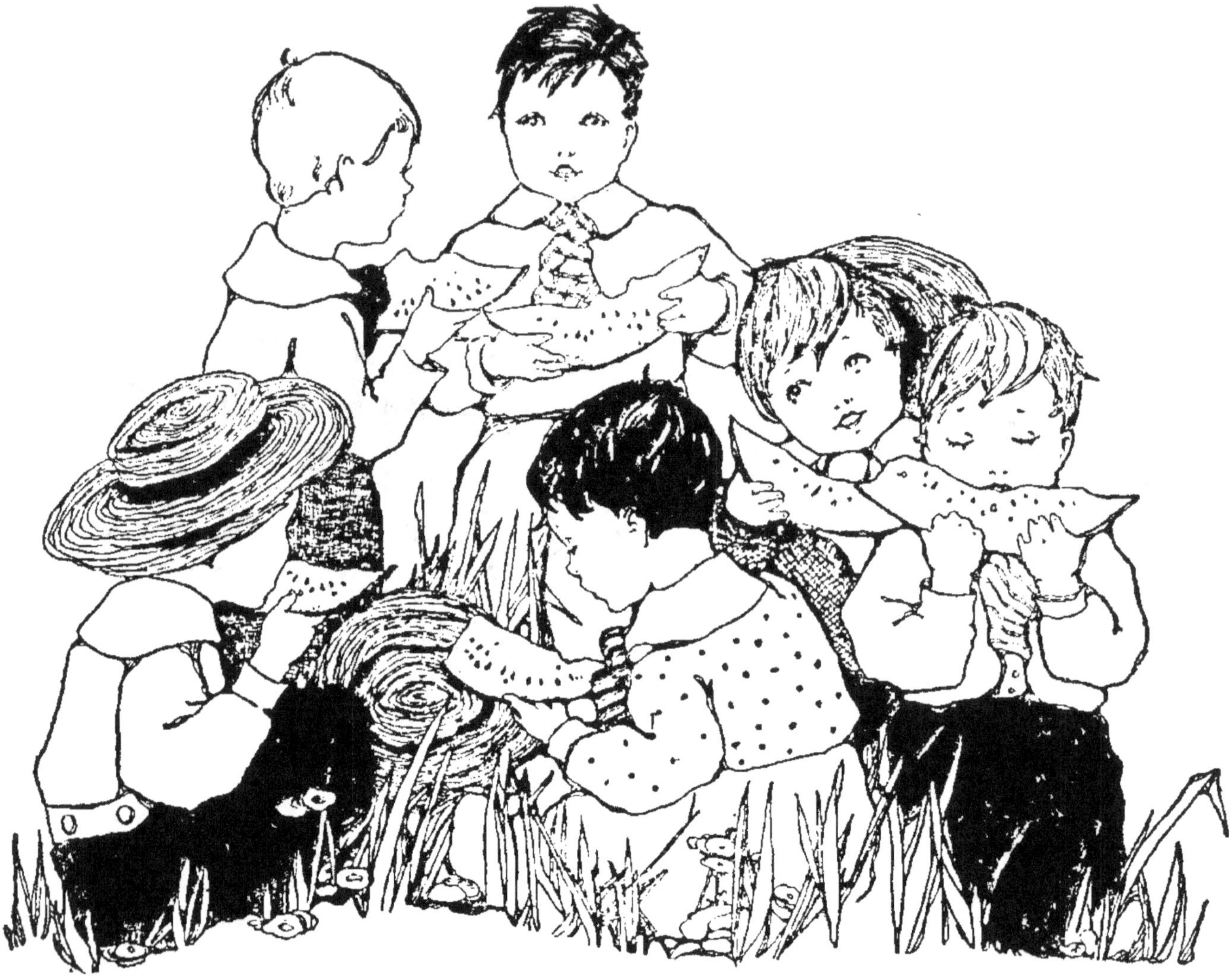

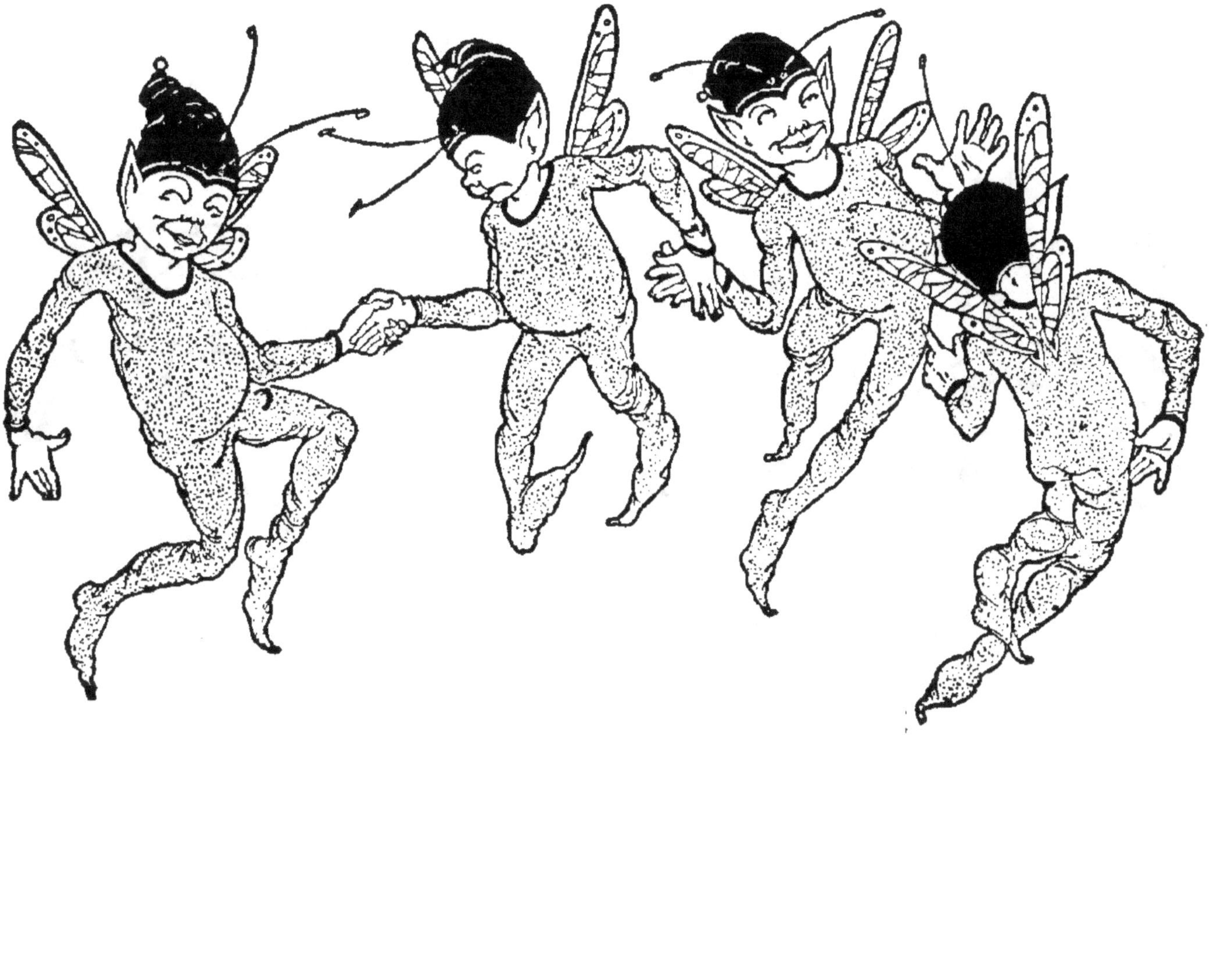

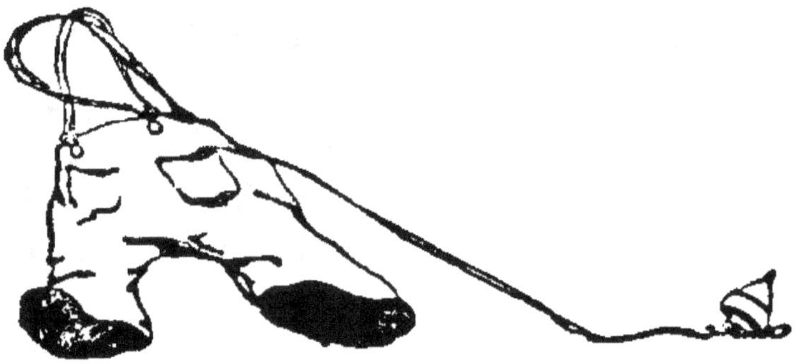

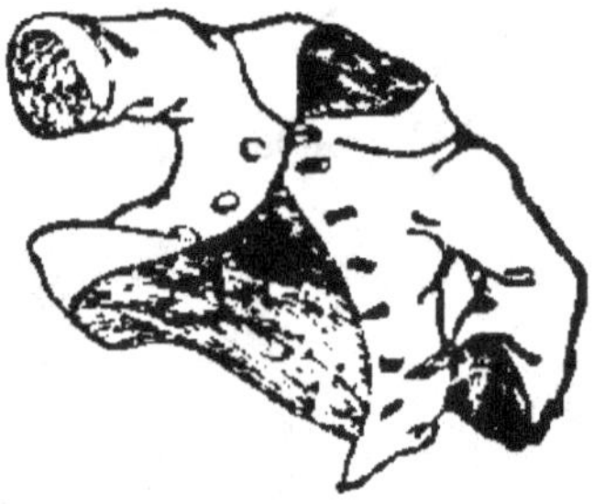

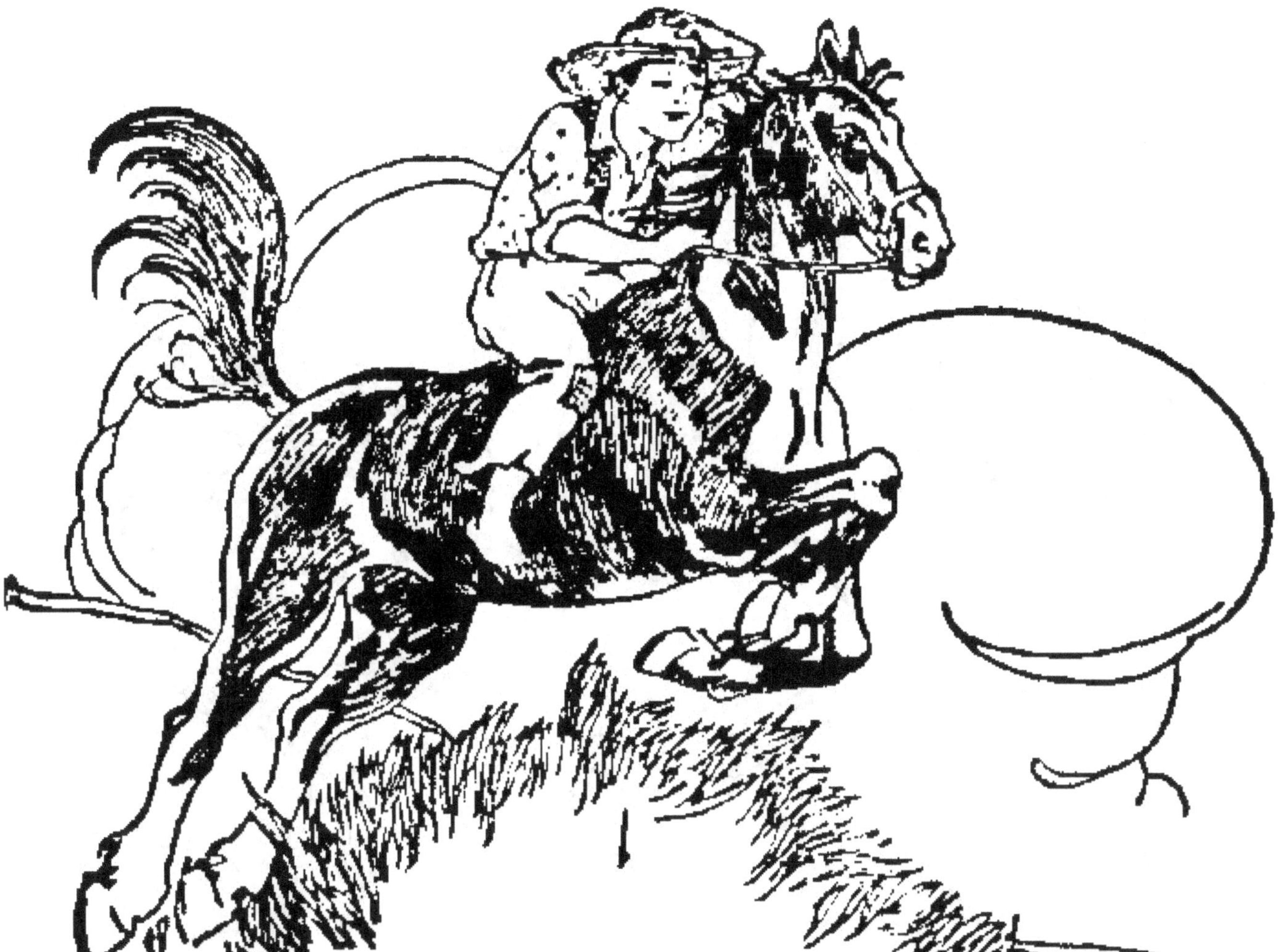

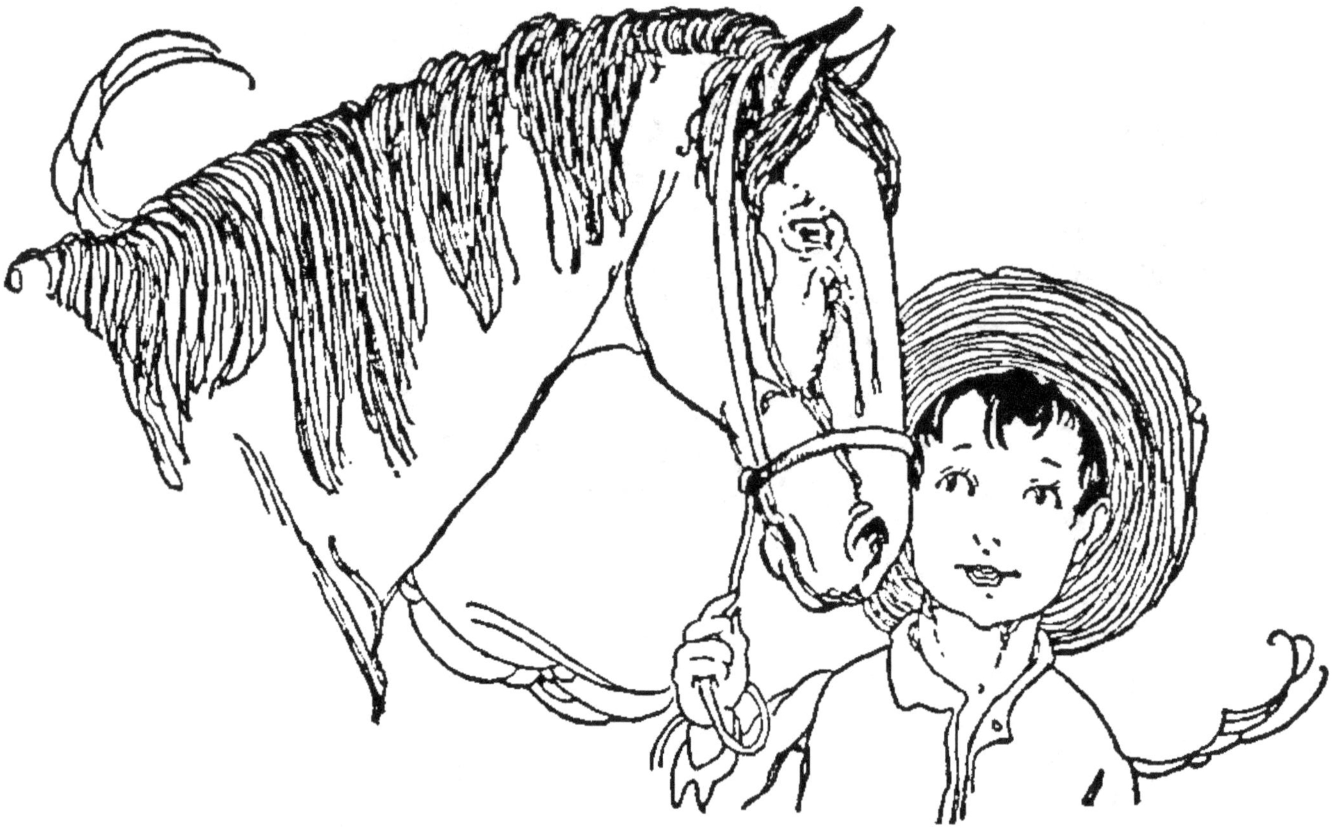

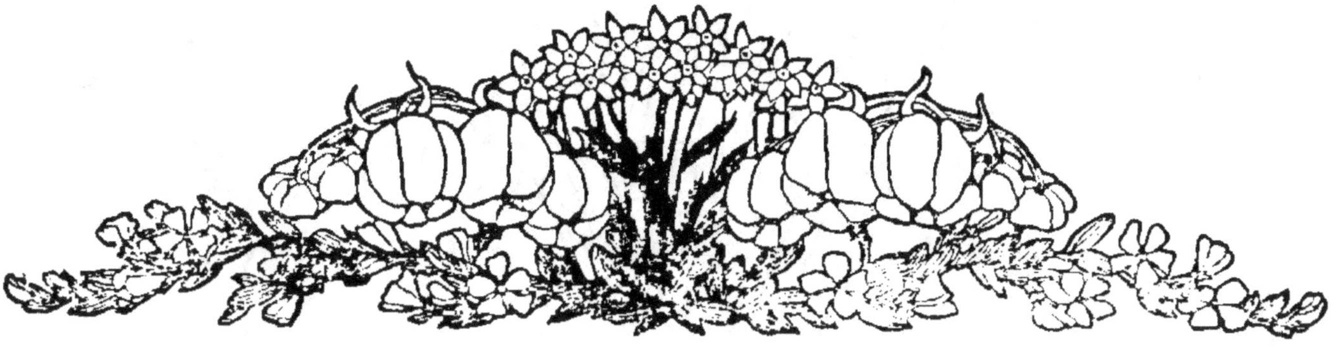

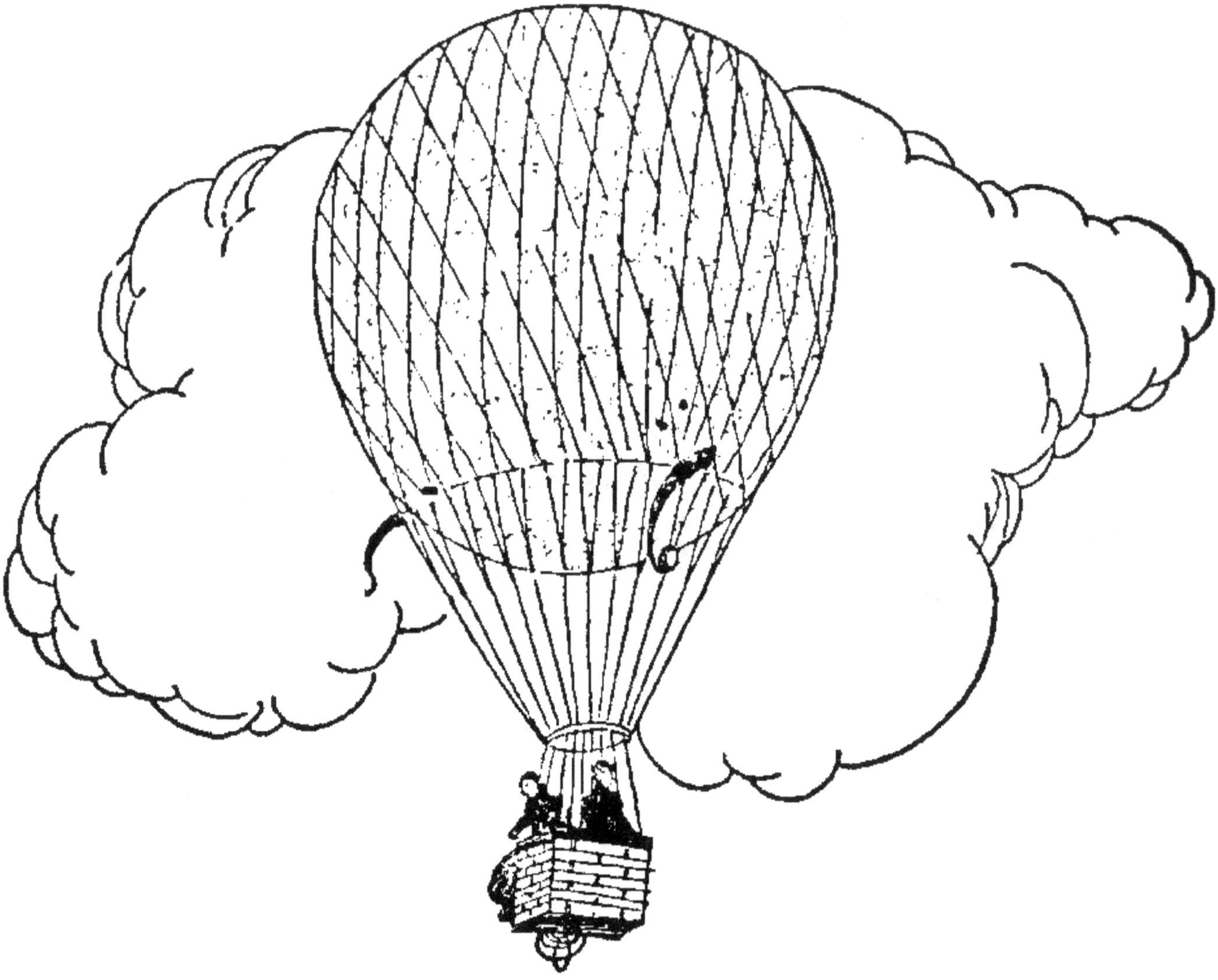

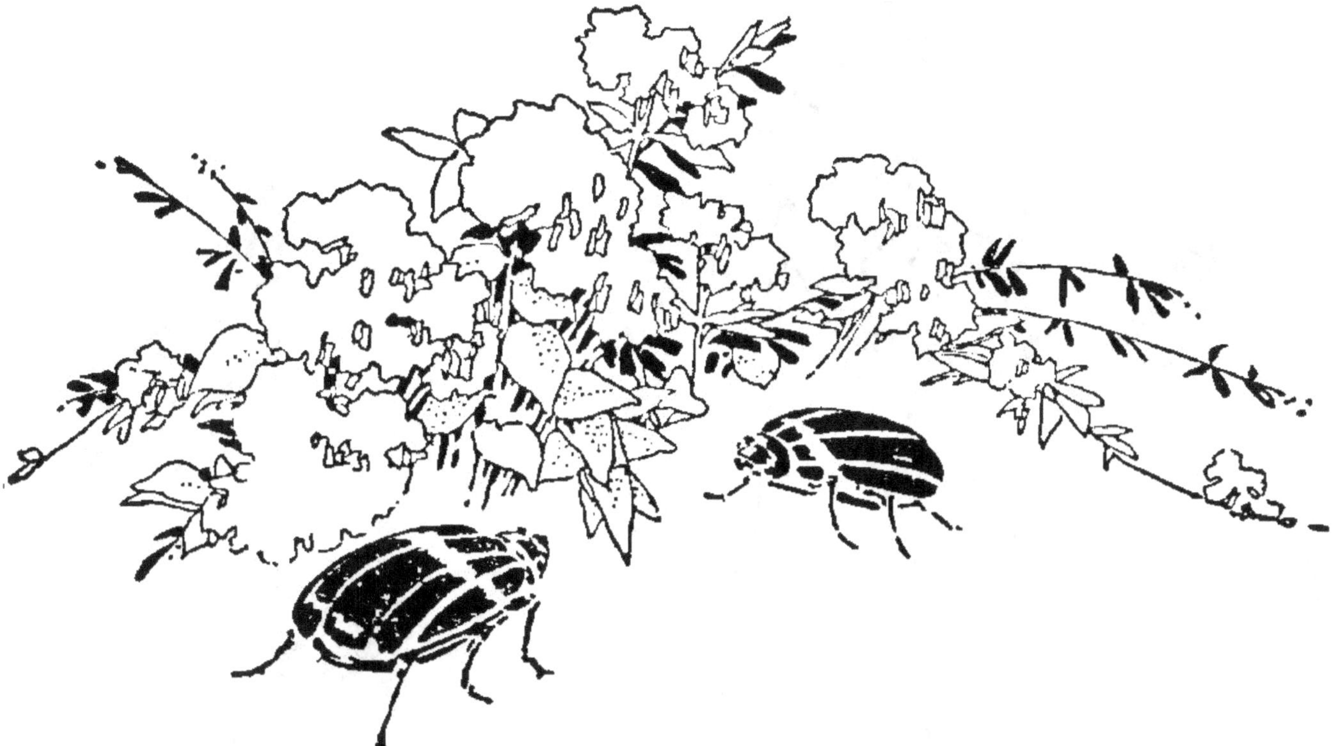

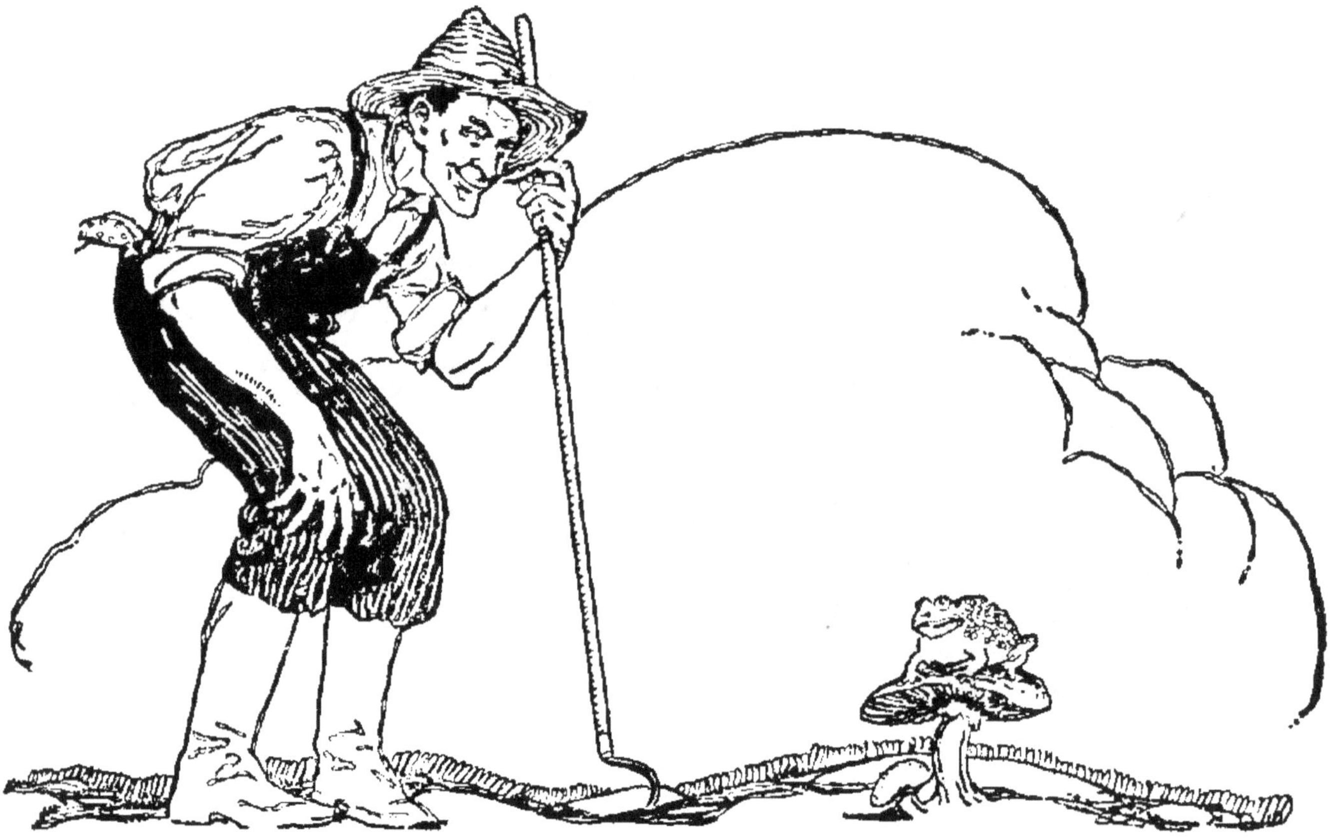

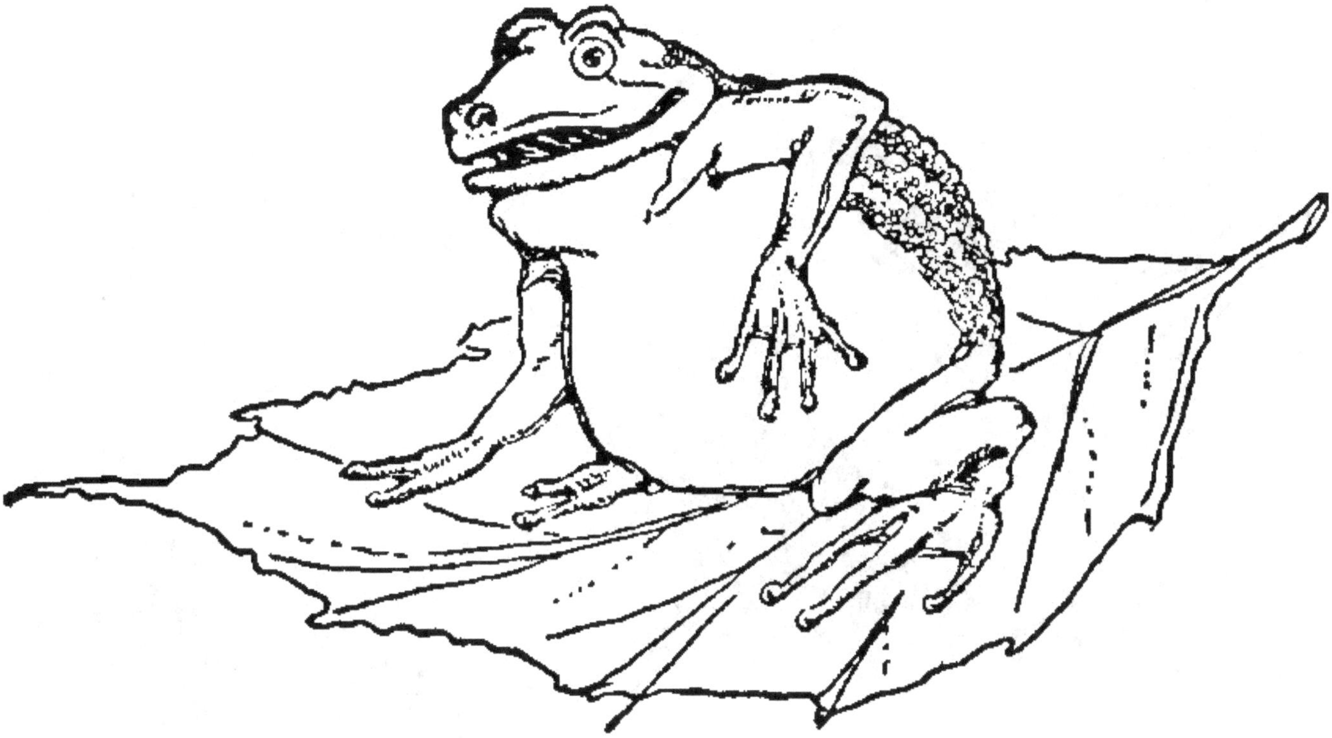

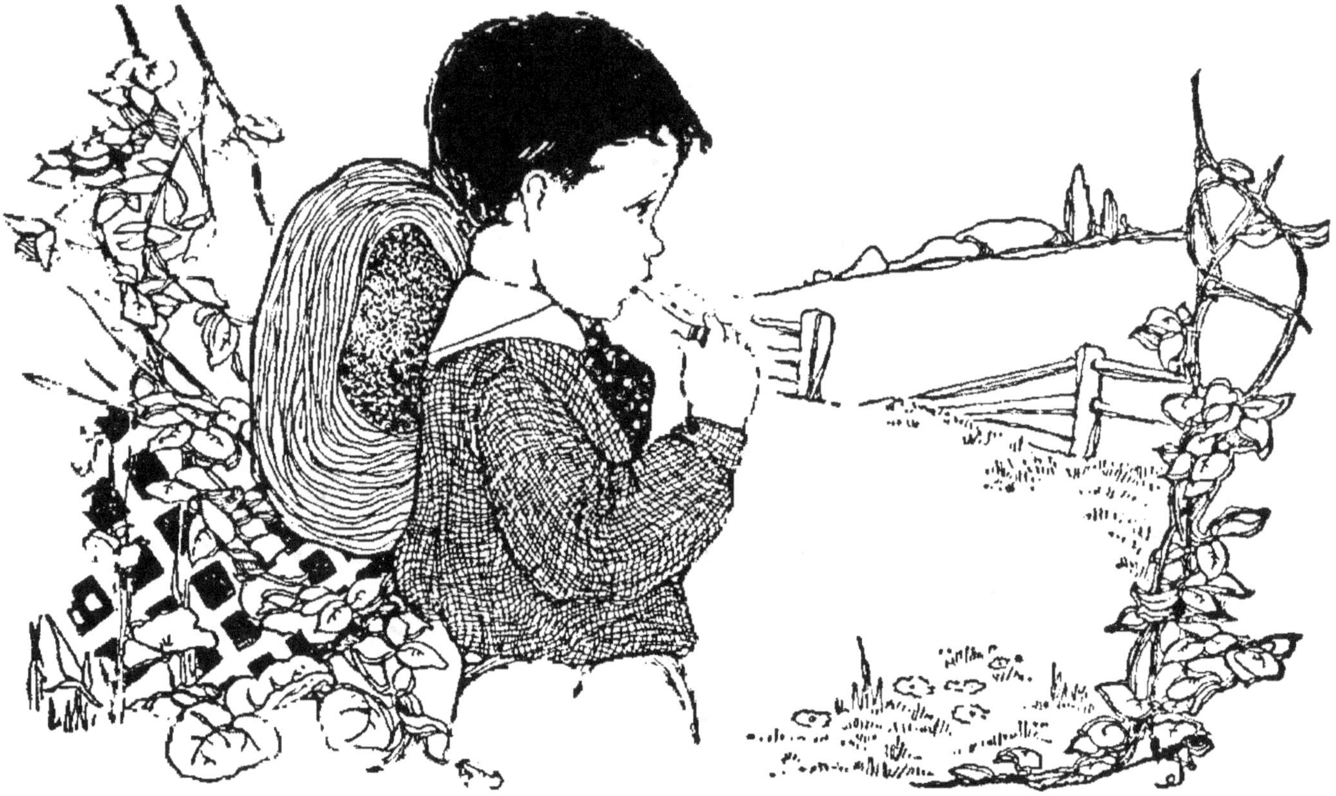

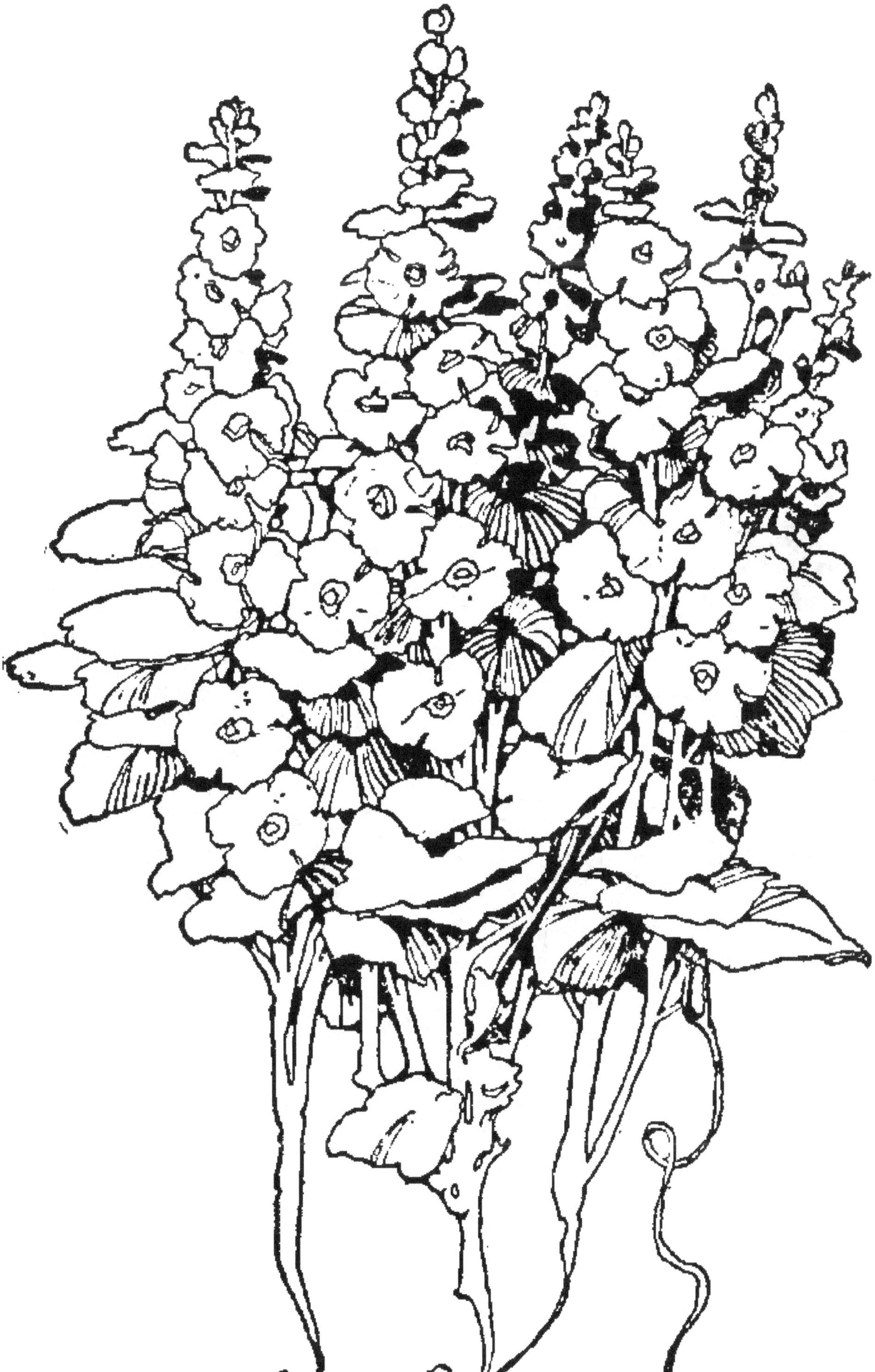

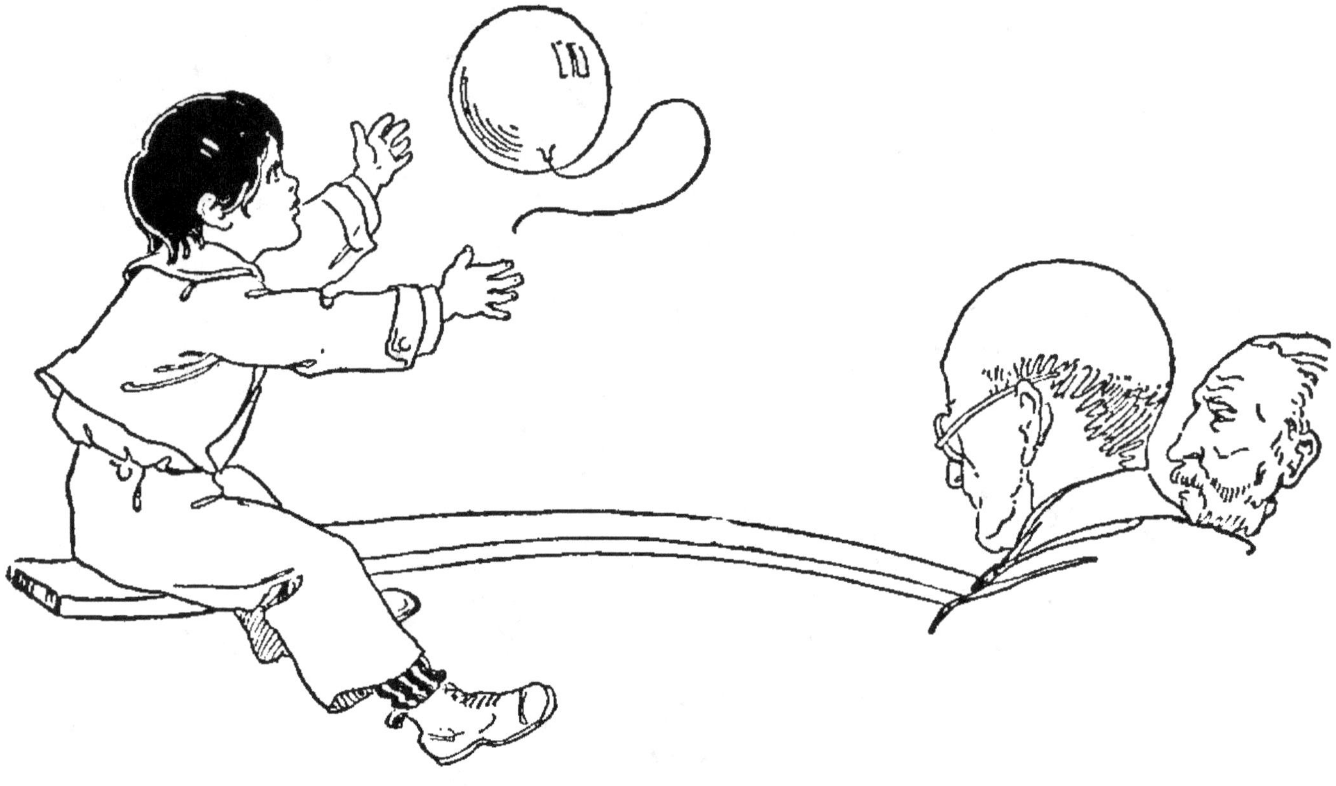

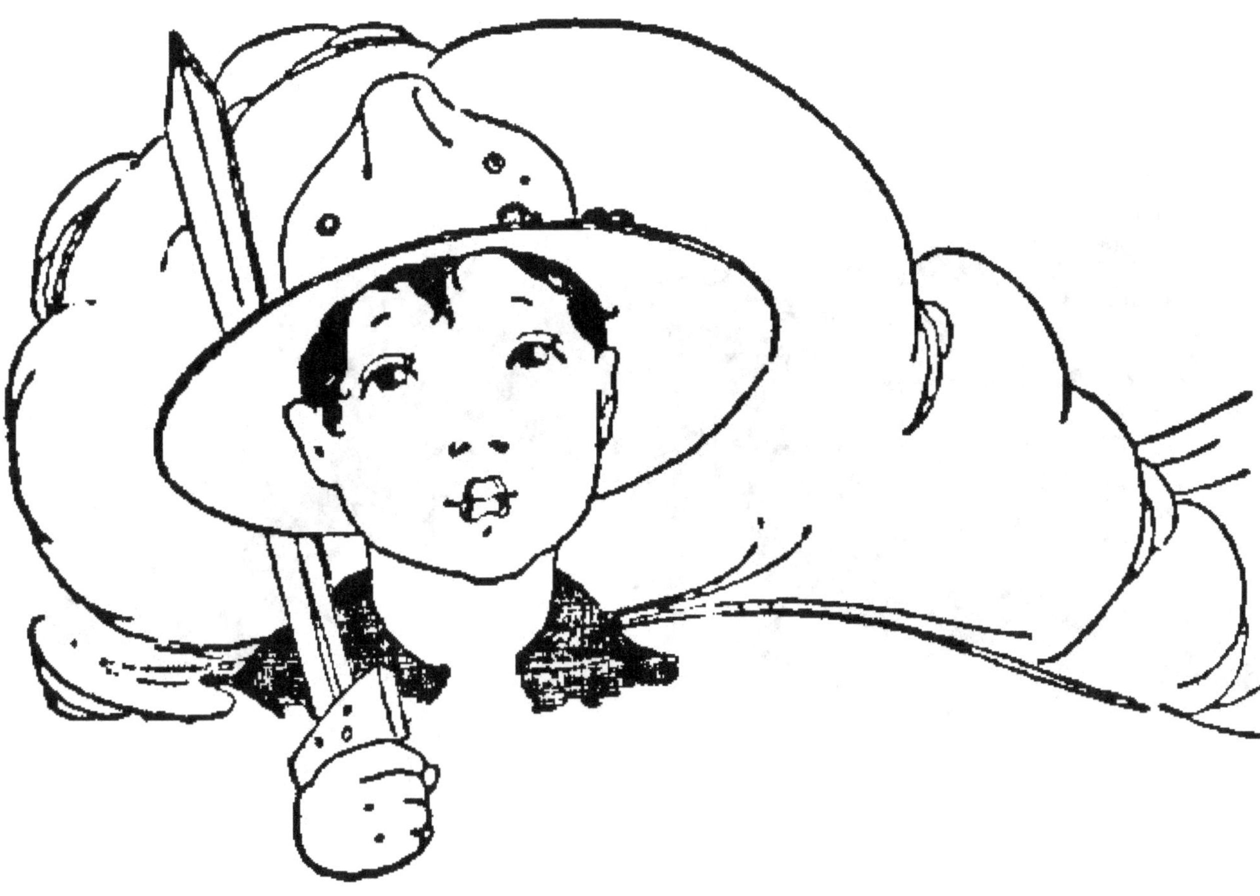

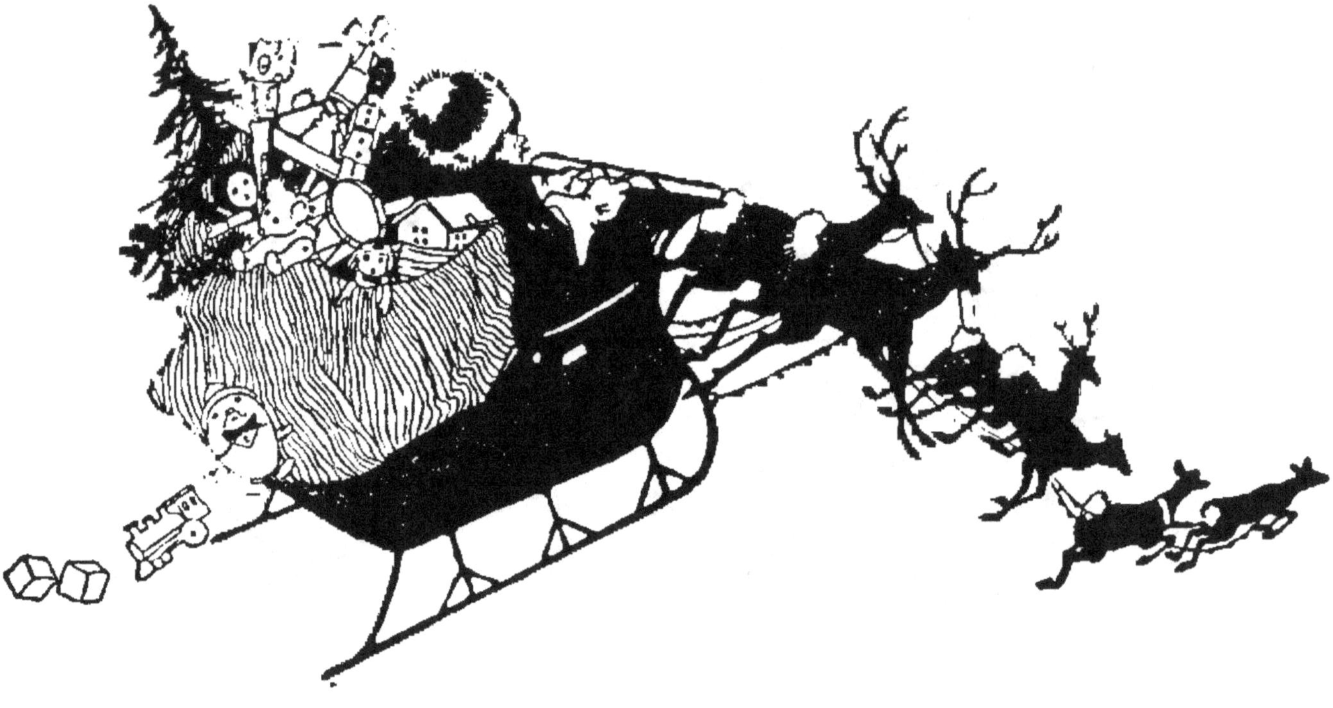

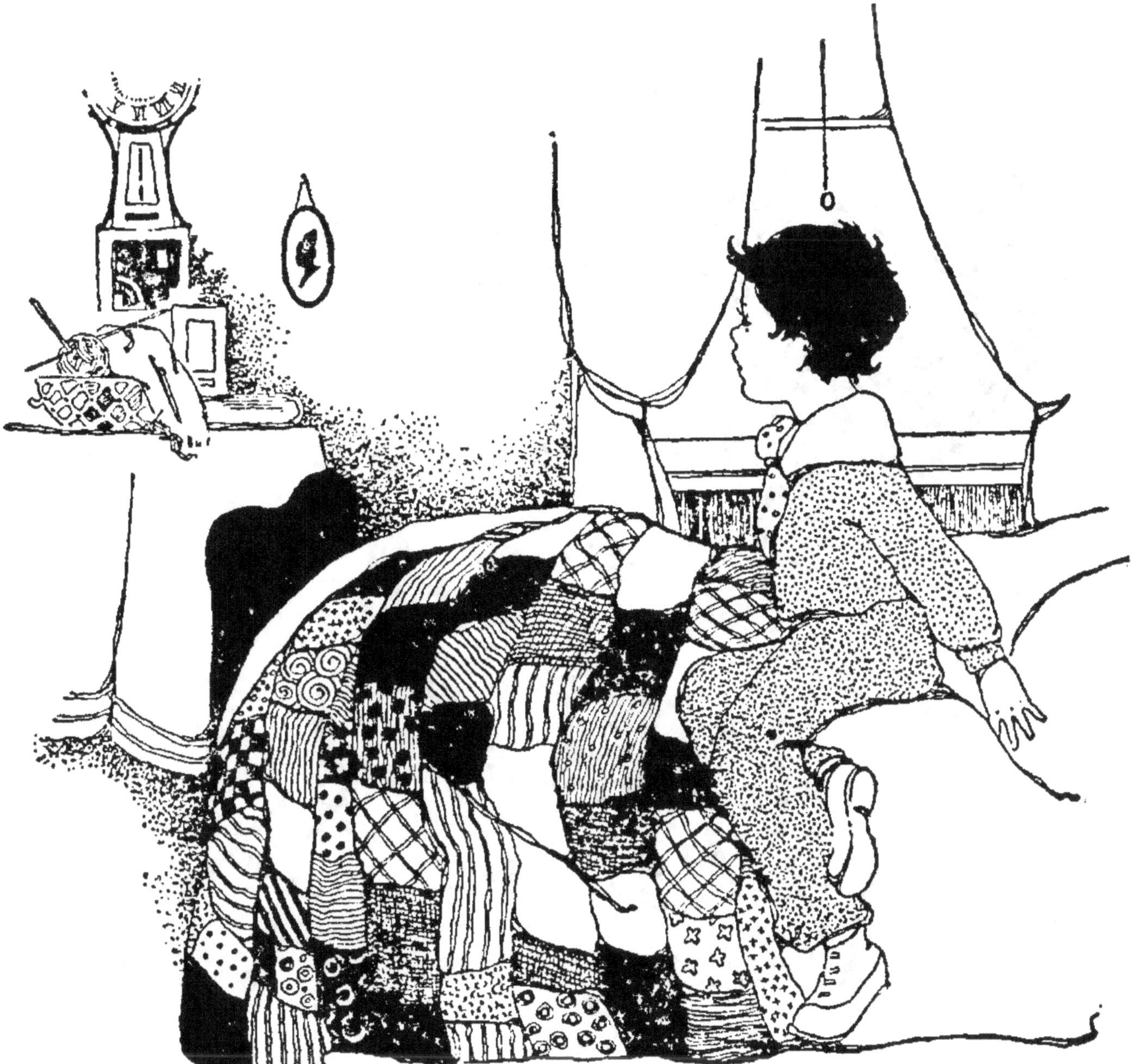

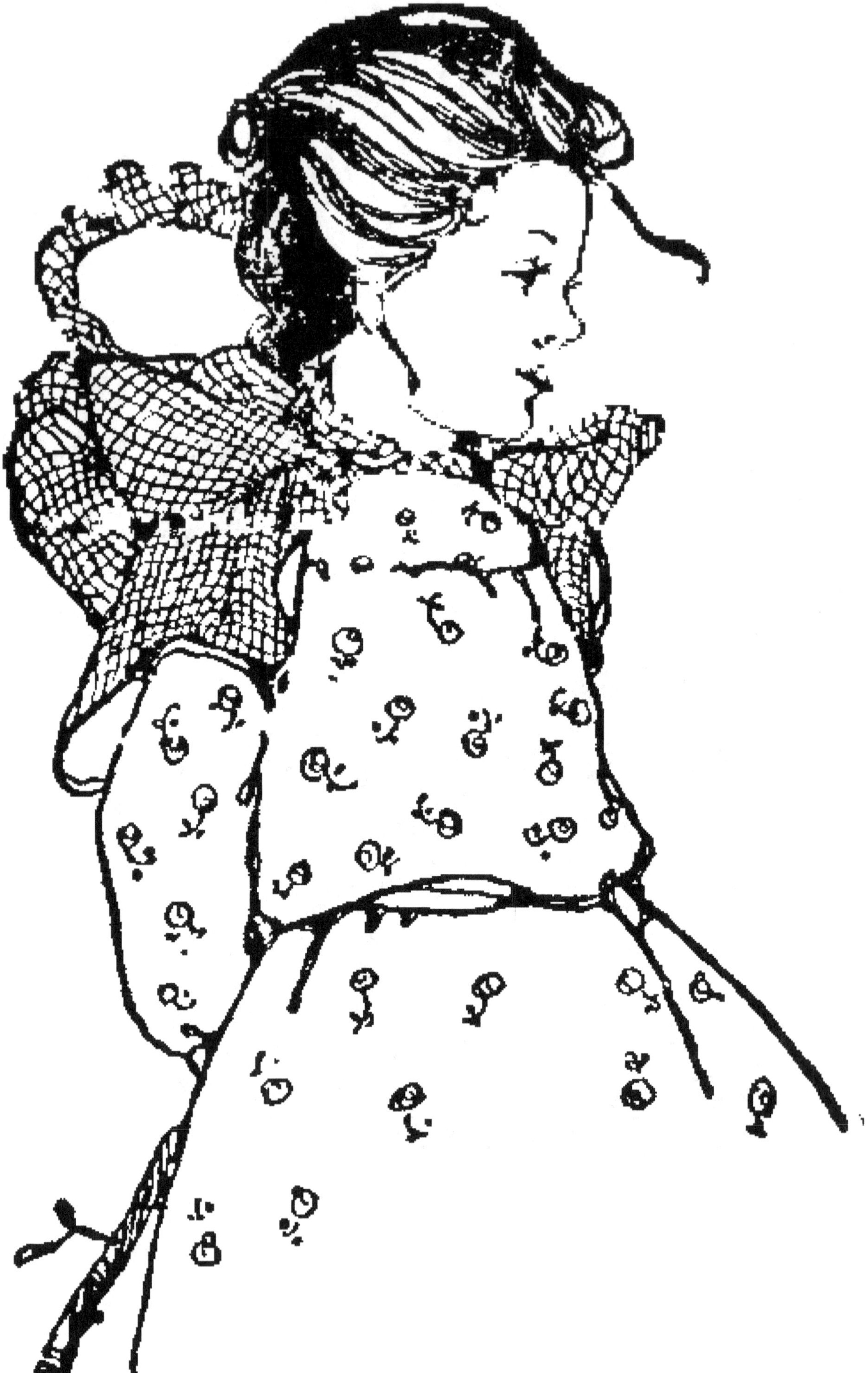

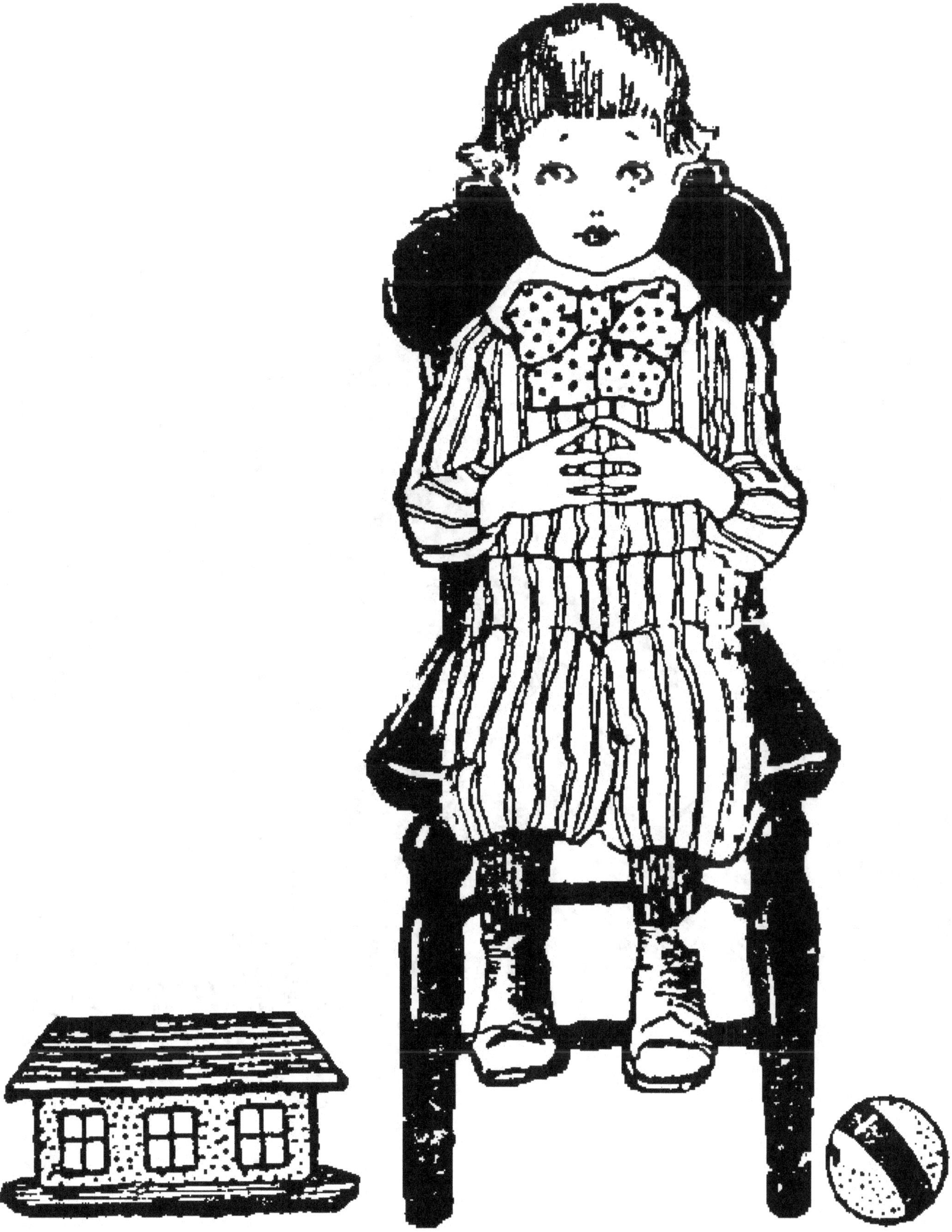

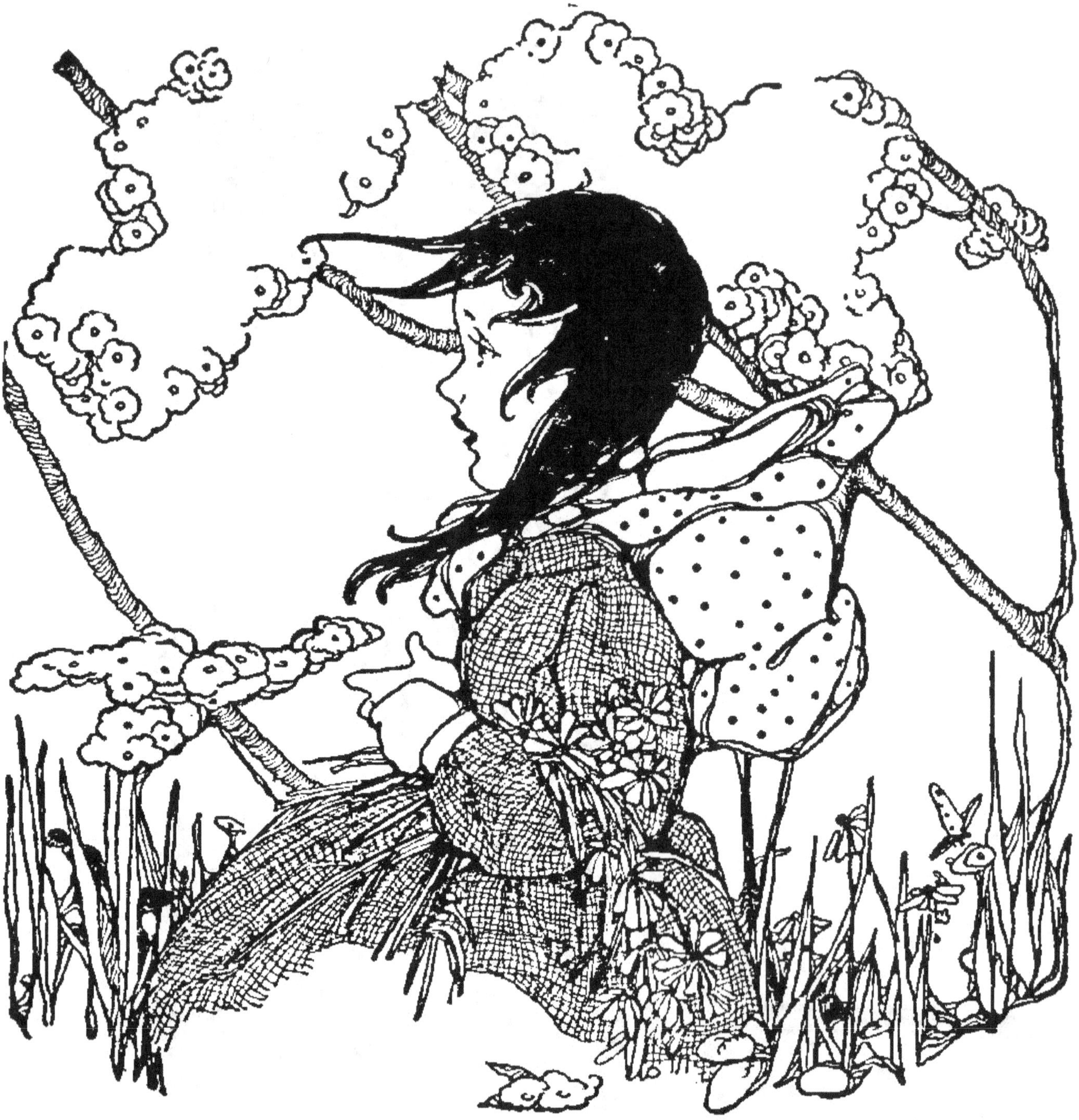

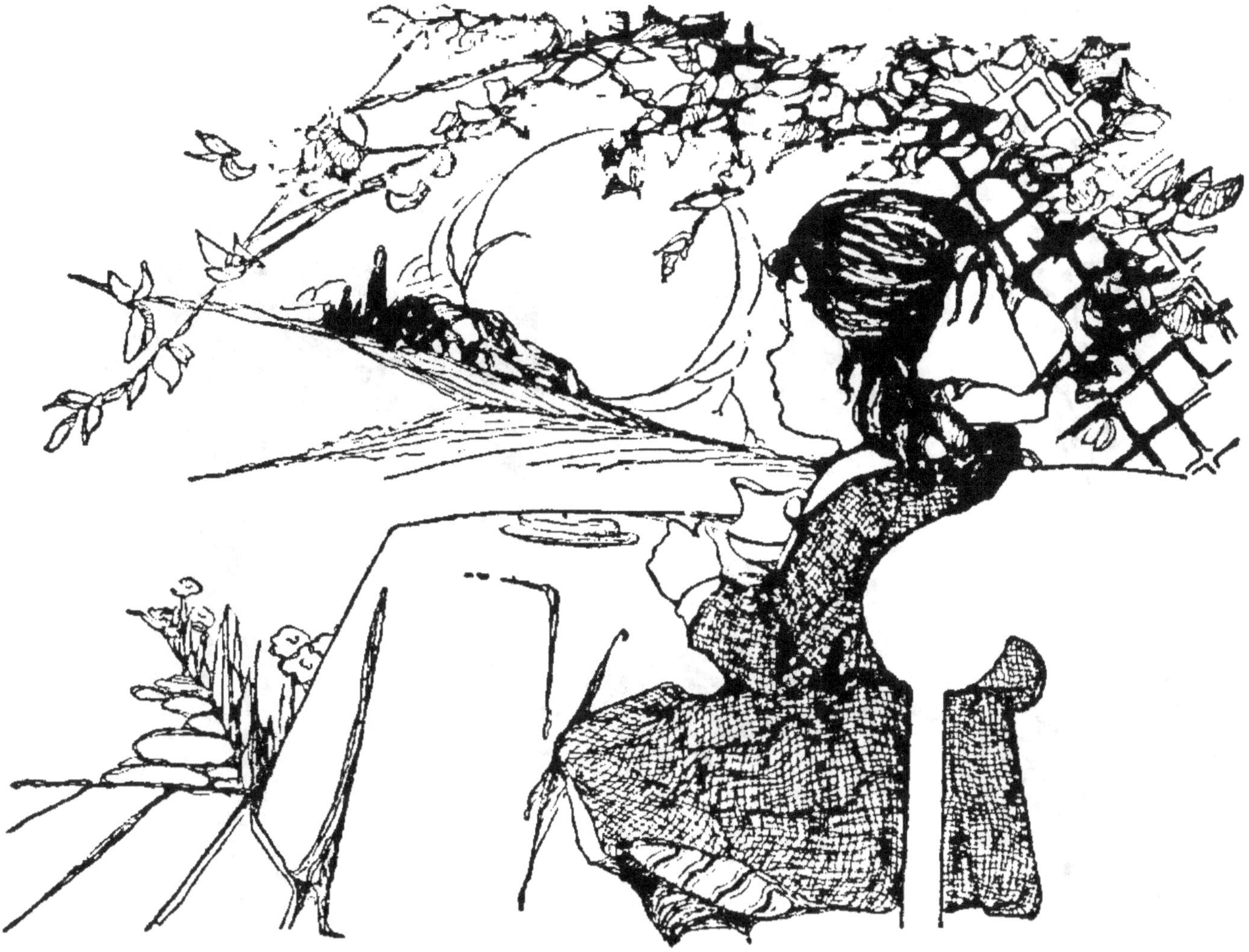

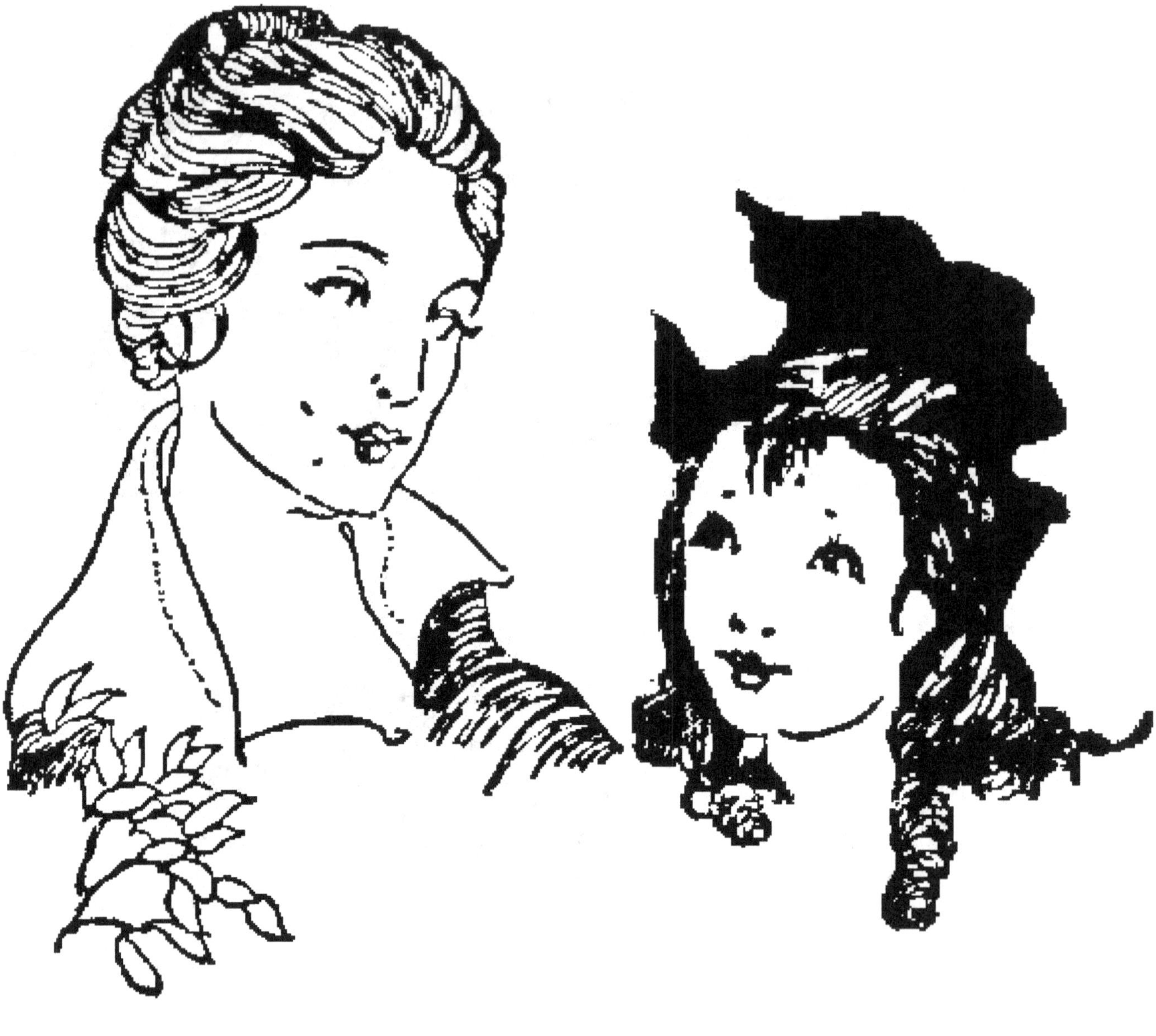

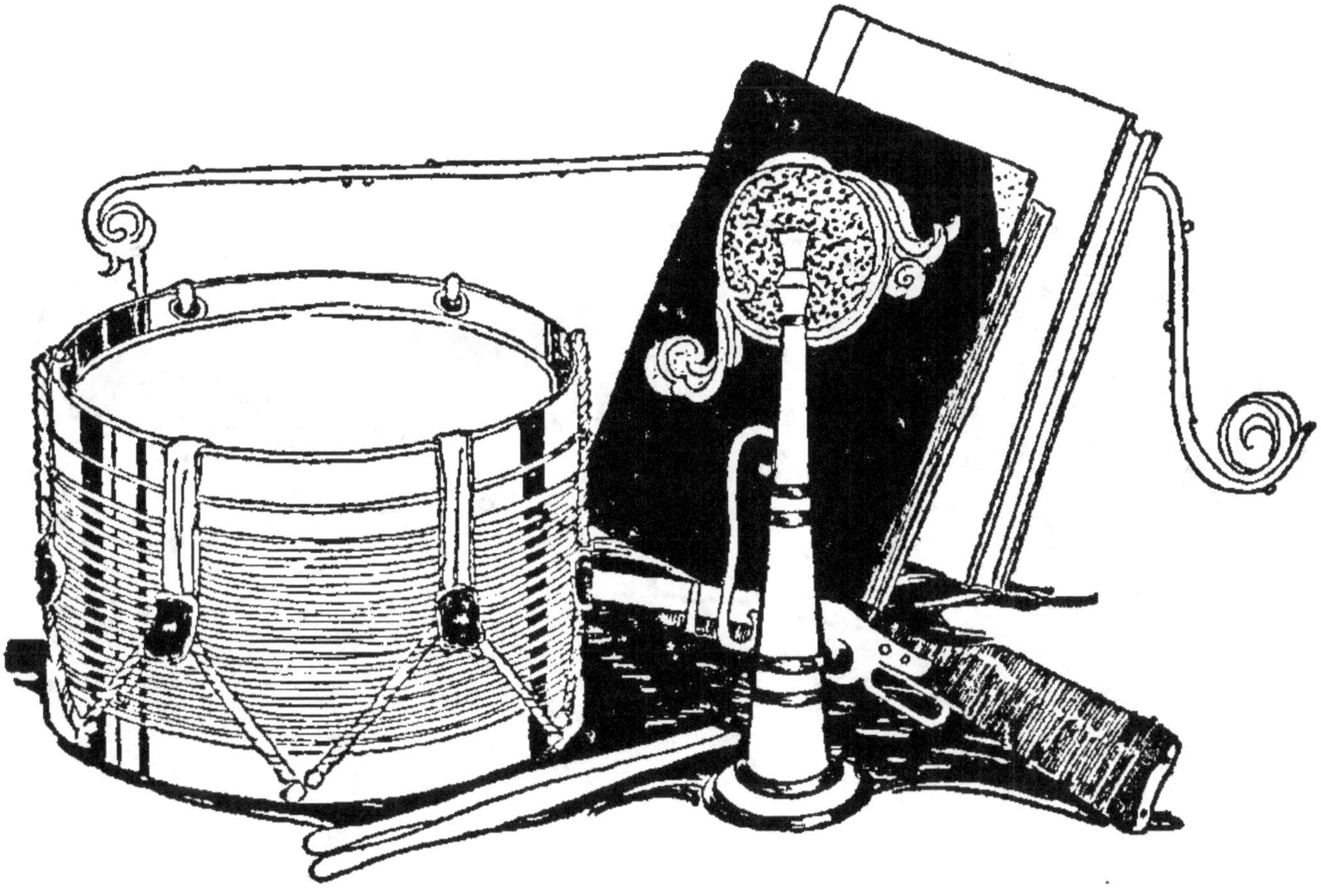

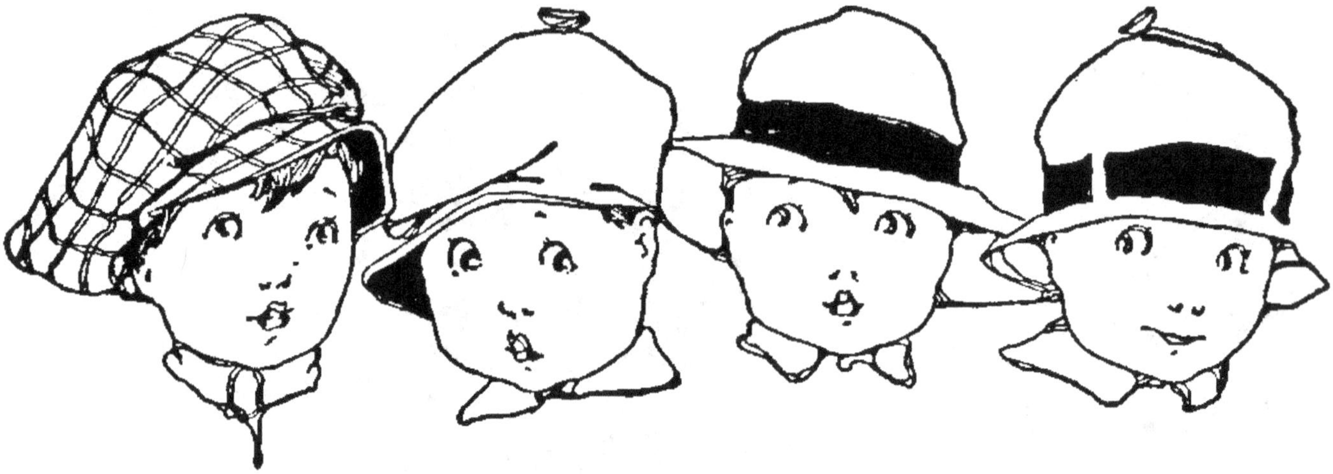

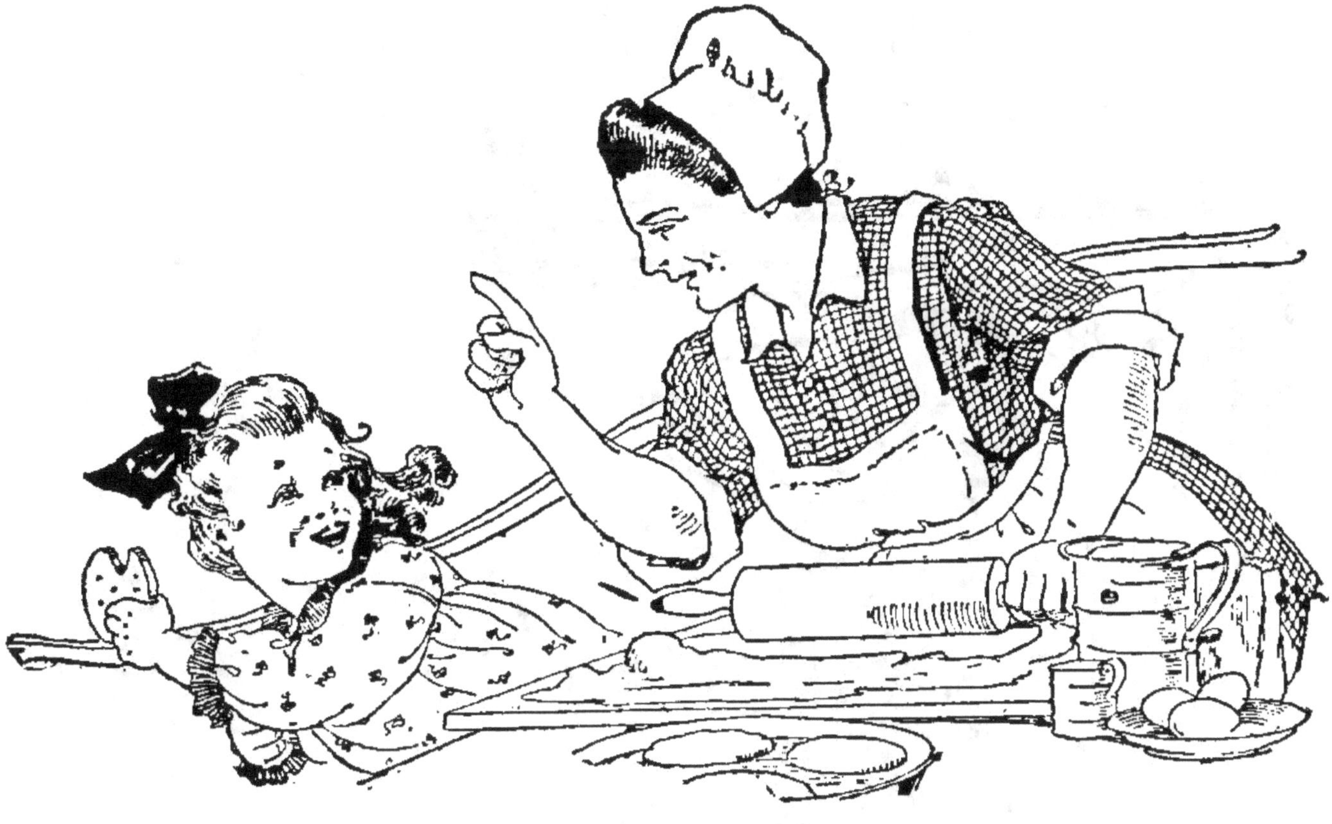

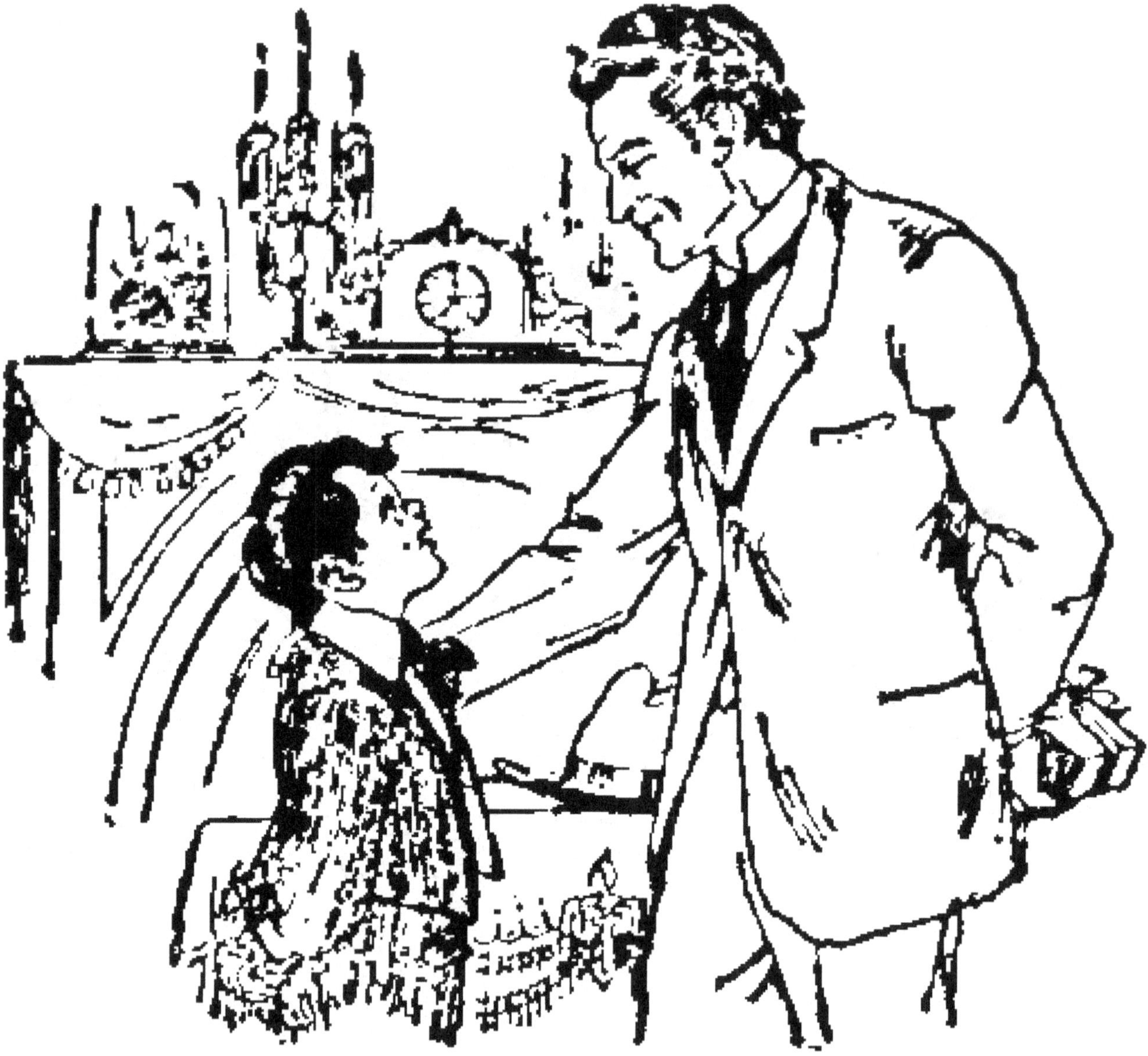

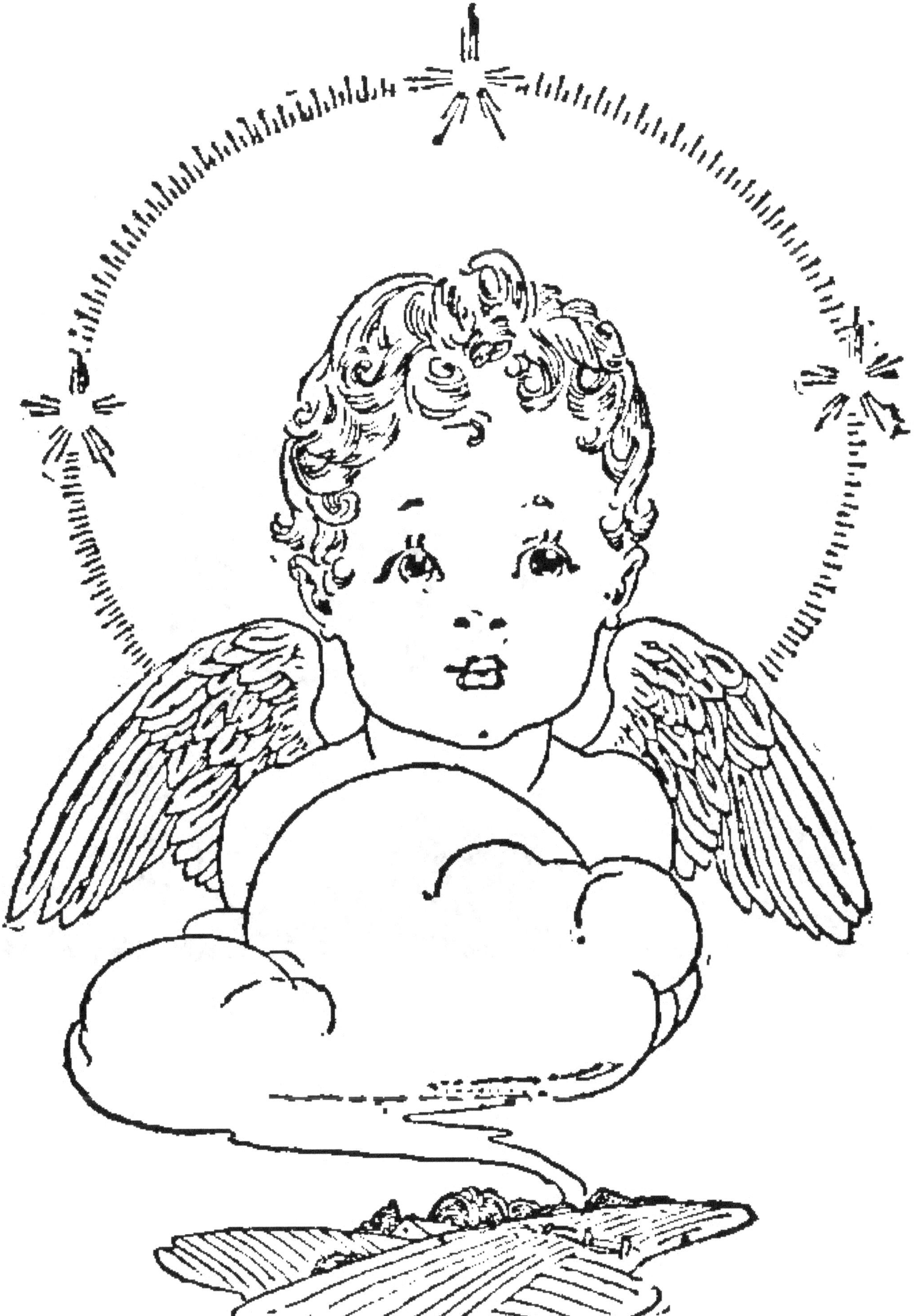

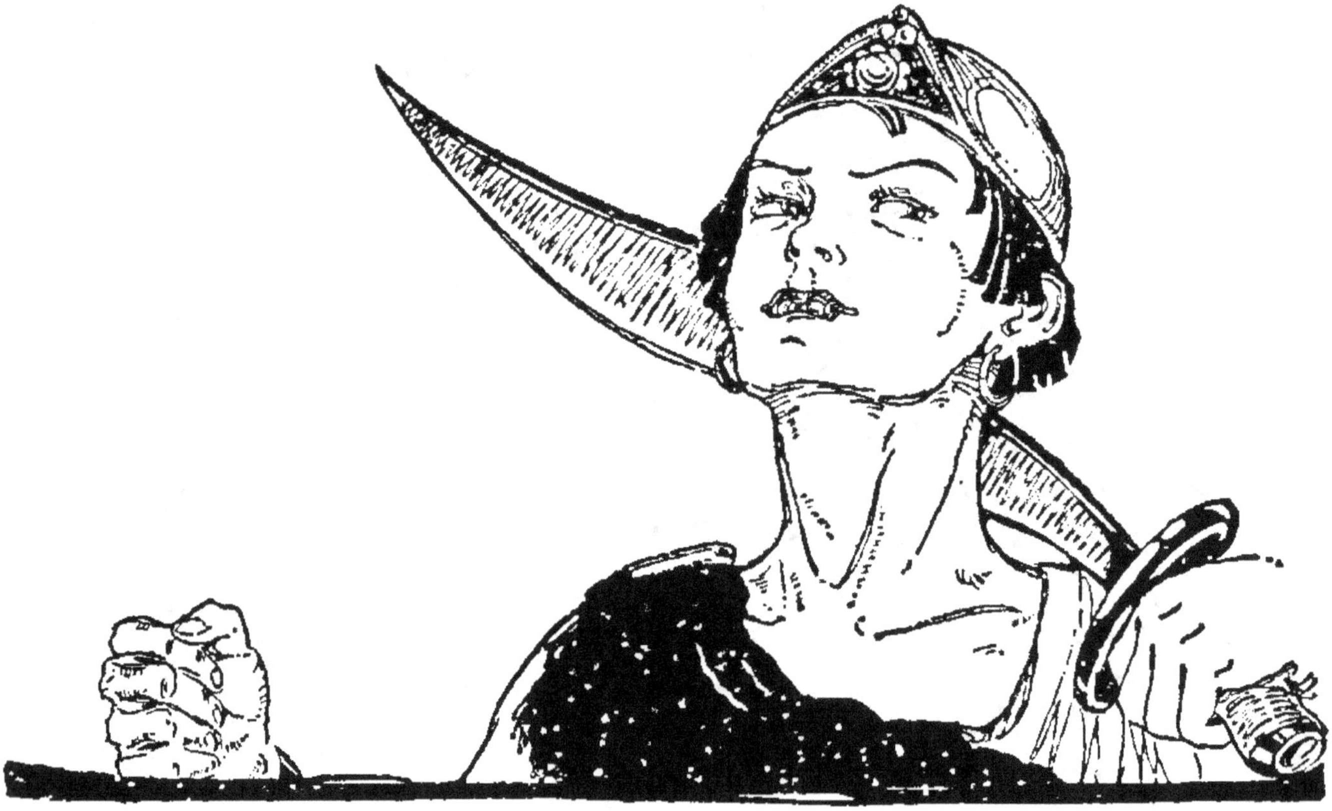

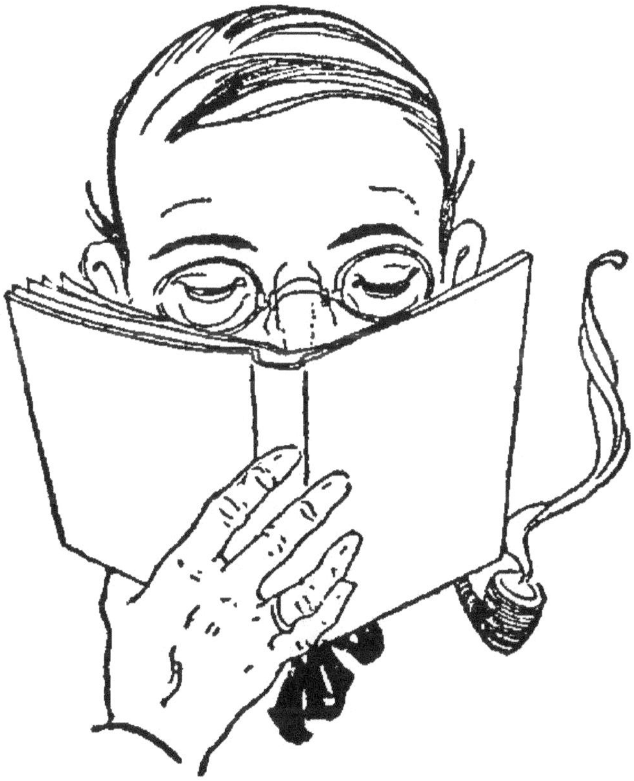

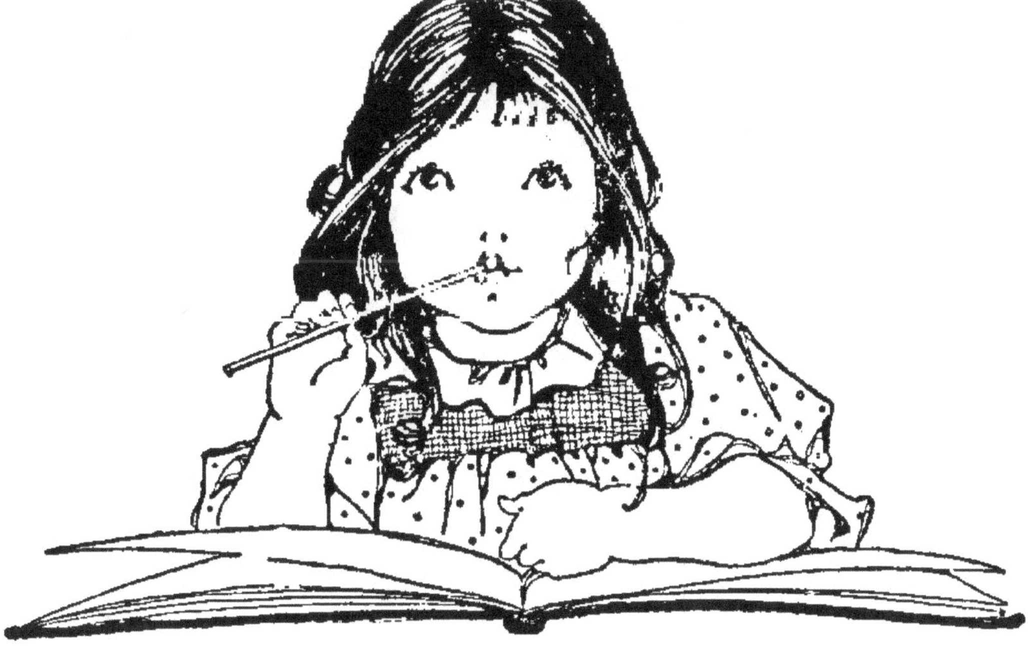

www.ingramcontent.com/pod-product-compliance
Lightning Source LLC
Chambersburg PA
CBHW081607220526
45468CB00010B/2805
* 9 7 8 1 7 2 3 4 2 0 3 0 6 *